The Book of Light

The Nature of God
The Structure of Consciousness,
And The Universe Within You

Volume One - Air

Consciousness is the Root of All Things

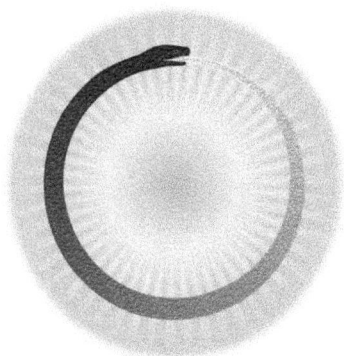

The Book of Light

The Nature of God
The Structure of Consciousness,
And The Universe Within You

Volume One - Air

Dr. Michael Sharp

www.michaelsharp.org

The Lightning Path

www.thelightningpath.com

Lightning Path Press

St Albert, Alberta. Canada

www.lightningpathpress.com

Library of Congress Cataloging-in-Publication Data
Sharp, Michael, 1963-

The Book of Light   / by Michael Sharp.
p. cm.
Includes index.

ISBN-13: 978-0-9738555-2-4 (v. 1 : pbk. : alk. Paper)
ISBN-13: 978-0-9738555-3-1 (pdf glassbook)
1. Spiritual life--Miscellanea. I. Title.

BF1999.S437 2006
204'.4—dc22
2005032547

Row, row, row your boat
gently down the stream,
Merrily, merrily,
merrily, merrily
Life is but a dream

Table of Contents

Note to the Preface

The book that you have in your hand is the first of a four volume series of revelation.[1] This series "reveals" the nature

---

[1] I use the word revelation here to represent the expression of truth acquired through internal exploration and reflection, through mystical exploration and connection with what I call the Fabric of Consciousness. When one has a mystical experience one connects to the Fabric and truth (often represented as *noesis* in the psychological literature) is revealed. When one writes about these experiences, when one presents the noetic truths, one is engaged in a process of revelation. One is "revealing" to oneself, and the world, what one has apprehended through connection with the Fabric of Consciousness. Often there is an assumption by some people that revelation is necessarily an accurate representation of high level spiritual truths. One thus reads the Old Testament of the Bible, or the *Sepher Yetirah* of Jewish mysticism, as divine and sacrosanct revelation. We then find centuries of scholarship aimed at trying to understand what is assumed to be a noetic masterpiece of divine revelation. There is no such assumption in my writing. Revelation refers to the process of realization and expression of noetic truth, but it does not speak to the accuracy of the truth. One can access revealed knowledge, but lack of a sensible scientific or conceptual foundation, psychological dysfunction, emotional immaturity, intellectual naiveté, political or economic interests, and a host of other mitigating factors can corrupt the revelation and/or presentation. It is a basic epistemological problem, and one that will be familiar to epistemologists. It is a problem in science; it is a problem in mysticism. Indeed I would argue it is more of a problem in mysticism because in mysticism there are, currently, no valid epistemological tests against which to compare a specific revelation. Scientists can point to empirical verification, mystics can only point to the ideas in their head. This is not exactly a firm ground to develop a solid revelatory understanding of creation. Bias, self-interest, political interest, economic greed, and even confusion covered over in veneers of arrogance are all part of the mystical

of consciousness, the nature of physical creation, and our human relation. The book is based on the mystical experiences of me, Michael Sharp. Two sections of this book, the following preface, and appendix one, provide an academically oriented discussion of the mystical experiences and cosmological and theological revelations provided in the main body of this book. If you are not familiar with academic research on mystical experience, if you are not familiar with other mystical texts, if your primary interest is mystical revelation and not scientific analysis, or if you find the information in the preface and appendix too thick and dry, feel free to skip over them and jump right into the introduction and revelatory part of the book. The information provided in the two sections is absolutely unnecessary to understand the cosmology and theology outlined in the mystical meat of this four volume series. In fact, in a certain sense, the information in the next two sections may make appreciation of the mystical core of this book series more of a challenge. Mystical experiences are grounded in right brain activity, and the linguistic and temporal lobe functioning of the left brain tends to dominate and pre-empt the softer, more artistic, holistic, and mystical

---

landscape. Does this necessarily invalidate revelatory knowledge? I don't think so. Nevertheless attention has to be paid to epistemological and methodological considerations, and critical space has to be maintained whenever one views revelatory knowledge. I would not be the one to throw out the baby with the bathwater, but I would certainly be the one to point out when the water is filthy and dirty. Although I won't have space to say too much about the epistemology and methodology of mysticism in this book, I will jot a few notes down, and make a promissory note to go into more detail at a later date.

side of your brain.[2] Reading the next two sections will activate your left brain and put you in an intellectual space not necessarily conducive to appreciating the writing that follows. It is best, therefore, to read the preface and appendix separate from the body, at least at the outset, and especially if your mystical experiences are absent, or immature. You can always come back and read the preface and appendix at a later period. Give yourself some time and space between exploratory academic materials, and follow the advice at the end of the preface about putting yourself in an appropriate emotional and psychological space. More than anything else the revelatory sections of this opus are meditative. This is so not only because of the nature of the writing (i.e. it is mystical) but also because of its depth and breadth as well. The deeper you get into the "emanation/Unfolding of Creation, the more the vistas of creation will expand in front of you. And let me tell you, the vistas are grand. If you want to fully appreciate the grandeur of creation, if you want to "connect the dots" and take what I have given you here and apply it to your own life and work, you'll need to go slowly. You need to give yourself some time and space to understand. Reading the mystical sections of this opus once through quickly, like you might read a scientific article, will not suffice. You'll need to meditate, and by meditate I just mean relax, slow your

---

[2] The significance of the right hemisphere in psychic phenomenon has been investigated by Don (2010, p. 117) who found a relationship between successful clairvoyant activity on the part of a known psychic Olof Jonsson, and "reduction or reversal of left hemisphere dominance as indicated by broad changes in EEG power."

thinking, read carefully each sentence, and ponder the truths being revealed. Getting into the proper "head space", and returning to that head space continuously, will increase your chances of properly apprehending the revelatory materials in this text.

Preface to Volume One

Before throwing you into the mystical meat of this book, I want to say a few things about this volume. First of all, the book you have in your hand, and this series in general, is intended to be a *non-denominational revelation*. That is, you should be able to see and recognize the truths represented here no matter what your particular spiritual, religious, or scientific background. In order to facilitate this non-denominational revelation, neutral language and concepts are developed. In particular several key spiritual terms are introduced and defined. For example, in this book I coin the term *Fabric of Consciousness* to describe the original conscious ground of creation. The term Fabric of Consciousness is intended to be a non-ideological, non-doctrinaire, easy to transport way of referring to what have otherwise been mystically obscured, poorly specified, and largely ungrounded concepts of consciousness. The details of the nature of the Fabric, and its relationship to physical creation, are developed in the course of this four-volume treatise.

The book is also intended to be an *open revelation* (as opposed to an esoteric obfuscation) of the mystical truths of consciousness and creation. That is, this book is written not for "the chosen," not for "the few," and definitely not for "the worthy," but for everybody, regardless of class, ethnicity, gender, and sexual orientation. At no point in the course of this unveiling are any claims to worthiness "invoked," nor is any testing required. You may have access to the high spiritual truths in this book no matter what your background, and no matter what you have done, and regardless of "test performance." Supporting this "open mysticism", in this book you will find no esoteric gobbledygook, no pretentious EPMO,[3] and no effort to veil or obscure. Everything is laid out in an easy to understand, easy to apply format. The concepts and answers provided in this book are specific, grounded, and clear and they should be relevant and satisfying to you no matter what your esoteric, spiritual or mystical background. Indeed if you have been a seeker of truth before then no matter what your background, you should find reflected in this Book of Light, in clear and unmuddied form, the spiritual, esoteric, and scientific truths you are familiar and comfortable with.

In the context of the above statements, this book (and this series) is intended as a sort of "key to the mysteries," a "book of light" that sheds light on (and thus "opens up") various mystical and religious traditions of the planet. Although this book does not participate in any specific exoteric, esoteric, or mystical tradition (indeed, it initiates a new one called the *Lightning Path*), you will find revealed in its pages the deep (and often esoteric and intentionally obscured) wisdom of established approaches. The book, for example, fits well within, and clearly reveals, western Christian wisdom. Christians will find not only a Biblically meaningful account of creation (both before and after God's statement "let there be light"), but also a cosmological outline of Christ's teachings, especially his statements about the potential of the Body to "power up" and ascend. After reading this book many of the concepts in the Bible (especially the New Testament), many of the gnostic texts (Robinson, 1988) and

---

[3] See http://www.thespiritwiki.com/index.php/EPMO

many of the statements and teachings of Christ, will come into clearer focus.

In addition to casting a resonating light on Christian doctrine, this book also reflects hermetic doctrine, and provides a key towards understanding the fundamental principles of Western hermetic philosophy. Consider the following. As (Dummett, Decker, & Depaulis, 1996) note in their discussion of the *Corpus Hermeticum*, for hermeticism:

> Nature is virtually a living organism with all parts interdependent; the universe owes its unity to the Mind of God; He created the material world in imitation of an ideal world in His intellect; His spirit pervades the material realm; His will exercised through a hierarchy of beings, ranging from angels down through humans to spirits within minerals (Dummett et al., 1996, p. 6).

Putting aside the obvious sexism in the above passage, it is a fair statement of hermetic philosophy. This book is the key to that philosophy, and by the end of the fourth volume you will understand the basic hermetic principles, the nature of the Mind of God, and the relationship of the material world to this mind. The words and concepts you use to understand "hermetic" principles will be different (we will use *Fabric of Consciousness* to replace the ideologically loaded word "God", for example), sexist references will be eliminated, and so forth, but the basic truth of hermetic mysticism will come shining through.

In addition to fitting into hermetic traditions, there is also an alchemical character to the book. The concern here isn't transmuting lead to gold, but in understanding how physical matter is a reflection of psychological -> spiritual -> divine processes. Throughout the course of this series the alchemical connections between the Fabric of Consciousness (i.e. the Mind of God) and physical reality are specified and developed. By the end of the series, the alchemical truths of creation will have been clearly specified, bringing alchemical wisdom into the 21st century in a way that dishonors neither the traditions themselves nor the science that has emerged since (in particular chemistry and physics). In a way, this treatise may be seen as salvaging the world of medieval alchemists, who were arguably "on to something" (Holmyard, 1957 (1990)) as they themselves connected with the Fabric, but who never properly grounded the knowledge, or were ever able to clearly specify it.

Nowhere is the nature of this book as "key to the mysteries" more clear than in the demystified and grounded understanding of the basic and well-known hermetic dictum

As above, so below

Those of you familiar with hermetic philosophy and alchemy will be familiar with the above dictum, stated originally on the Emerald Tablet (Holmyard, 1923) It is generally meant to indicate some sort of relationship between "God" and creation, God's will and creation, or humanity's role as a conduit for God's will. The actual meaning of the dictum can be hard to pin down, especially considering the fact that the puffery that often goes into attempts to explicate this dictum knows no bounds (Holmyard, 1957 (1990)), but all uncertainty and confusion is eliminated when considering my corrected, unveiled, and properly grounded version of the dictum:

As above in consciousness,

So below in matter.

To be perfectly clear, I view my restatement of the hermetic dictum as the *proper* way to state this high level, and extremely important "alchemical" spiritual Truth. Although there may be some ambiguity and uncertainty in your understanding of this principle now, let me assure you that by the end of even this volume you will have a clear, concise, and hard–to-shake understanding of the deep meaning of this "Sharp" restatement of the famous hermetic dictum. This will be true even if you have considered and previously adopted the older version of this dictum "as above, so below," as well. The restated dictum, and the revelation in this book, will clarify, ground, and enhance your understanding of this very important spiritual principle. Indeed I will even go so far as to state that by the end of this series you will understand the full meaning and import of the Emerald Tablet (which to be honest with you is not that particularly noteworthy or spectacular) much better than anyone who has not read this *Book of Light*.

As broad and incredulous as it may be appearing at this point, The Book of Light also provides a window into Jewish mysticism, for example the *Sepher Yetzirah: The Book of Creation*,[4] and the Tree of Life. The *Sepher Yetzirah* (SY) is a Jewish account of creation. According *Sepher Yetzirah* (SY), creation emerges from the essence of G-d (or *Ein Soph*) in a

---

[4] A "short version" of the Sepher Yetzirah, translated by the well-respected Aryeh Kaplan, is available online. Search for "Sepher Yetzirah short version Aryeh Kaplan".

long emanation from source. The *Sepher Yetzirah:*

> ...teaches that a first cause, eternal, all-wise, almighty
> and holy, is the origin and the center of the whole
> universe, from whom gradually all beings emanated.
> (Kalisch, 2006 (1877))

This is exactly the message and teaching of this four volume Book of Light. The accounting of this book starts with the "first cause," the Source. It provides foundational statements about the nature of Source (of G-d) as awareness, compassion, and bliss and proceeds to develop an account of the *emanation* that is rooted in the fundamental nature of the almighty and holy G-d. It follows, in other words, the "flash of lightning" (Kalisch, 2006 (1877), p. 16) by which creation unfolds and proceeds. From the opening statement of this book, *Consciousness is the Root of All Things,* to a representation of the "word of G-d" (not so much in twenty-two human constructed letters but) in the vibratory character of physical creation in volume three, to a description of the Sephiroth (named in this book "dimensions" of physical creation, and refined to reflect more accurately the physical and psychological dimensions of existence), to the emergence of the advanced physical[5] in volume four, this Book of Light opens up the wisdom buried deep in the *Sepher Yetzirah.*[6] This Book of Light is really just

---

[5] Of which the human body is but one example.

[6] The four volume series of this Book of Light follows the sequence of emanation as represented in SY, from Air to Water to Fire to Ether or Earth.

another version of the SY, but perhaps more worked out, grounded, and modern.[7] Indeed this entire book is nothing more than a description of the Lightning Flash of Creation as it winds its way from Crown (Fabric) to Kingdom (Earth). Those familiar with Jewish mysticism will find familiar ground here.

Finally, we may also point in the direction of Hegel (Hegel, 2004). Hegel had the view that behind history there was a Spirit (God essentially) and this Spirit expressed its essential nature through the unfolding of history. History was, according to Hegel, moving toward and end point and this end point was the realization of God in nature. Hegel's view, while focused exclusively on human history (and slightly Catholic and ideological in its presentation of "freedom" as the essential nature of God), nevertheless is compatible in broad outlines with the basic thesis of this Book of Light which is that the Unfolding of Creation occurs according to, the nature of consciousness, and in response to the problem of ennui. We will explore the Unfolding of Creation in the context of the evolution of the physical body, and the unfolding of human history, in volume four of this series.

In any case, those of you trained in other traditions may note correspondences between The Book of Light and your own past spiritual training. Whatever background you come to this

---

[7] You will note that the "tree of life" used on the cover of volume one of this series is highly Kabalistic in nature, though I would prefer to rename the Tree of Life the Tree of Lights to more properly reflect the monadic glory of the Unfolding of Consciousness, and the true source of the "emanations" into physical reality.

book with, I should note that you will not necessarily find a one to one correspondence. The Book of Light is not concerned with mapping all the various traditions into a single holistic tapestry (as some 19th century occultists tried, and failed miserably, to do). Rather The Book of Light is intended to provide just enough detail so that "light" may be shed on your particular tradition. Thus superfluous, poorly conceived, and/or corrupted concepts are dropped, [8] relevant concepts are clarified (sometimes redefined), and new concepts are added with a view towards enhancing inter-traditional commensurability. The result at the end is not a mere reflection of what has come before, but an update and purification of what is already there. In The Book of Light, the chaff is thus separated from the wheat.

It is useful to note in this context that the language used in The Book of Light, because the book itself is intended to be a general statement of high spiritual Truth, is more informal and light than a longtime student of spirituality, mysticism, and even the occult might come to expect. This may cause some to question the significance and depth of what is presented here. Rest assured, however, that just because the language is clear, grounded, and simple does not mean that the concepts or ideas have been dumbed down or reduced in any way. In fact, exactly the opposite is probably the case. All

---

[8] There is a considerable amount of intentional corruption in spiritual teachings. Nowhere is this made clearer than in the Freemasonic co-optation of the Western Tarot, and the imprinting of Masonic ideology onto the fabric of the system. See Sosteric (2013) *A Sociology of Tarot* for a detailed exposition of this. http://www.thelightningpath.com/halosharp/a-sociology-of-tarot/

this simply means is that I have spent more time thinking about how to express the concepts in a more appropriate manner than you would find in your typical mystical treatise. Mass understanding, communication, and complete revelation are the ultimate goals of The Book of Light. You cannot accomplish any of those goals whilst remaining tied to confusing grammatical turns, flowery language, and overly complicated prose (what I call EPMO) as sometimes represented in works of this nature.

Finally, I should note for clarity that this book is the result of the mystical exploration of me, the author, Michael Sharp. This mystical exploration is easy to specify, at least in the language of the Lightning Path. It occurs as I, the author, enter into a receptive state; connect my bodily consciousness with the Fabric of Consciousness, and "ground" or "download" information from the Fabric. The connection itself is straightforward and relatively easy to accomplish, but not unproblematic. A pure connection, a connection that allows the Truth to flourish, requires a clean channel through an undamaged vessel. The channel itself must be unencumbered by dogma, ideology, racism, sexism, and bodily ego and the vessel itself must be largely free of psychological damage and pathology. Anybody wishing to connect with the Fabric may do so, but anybody wishing to connect will do well to consider this: advanced spiritual experience, advanced spiritual work, and successful and uncorrupted connections to the Fabric (i.e. God/consciousness/spirit), are not a function of worthiness or tests or whatever else exclusionist hierophants may come up with to justify power, privilege, and inequality. Connection to the Fabric is simply a matter of psychological, emotional, and intellectual health, and purification and preparation of the vessel. Anybody with the discipline, time, and inclination, anybody with access to proper guidance, accurate information, and relevant support, can accomplish such a connection on their own. If one is worried about the accuracy and truth of the "revelations" contained in this Book of Light, the absolute best way to confirm them is to work toward advanced spiritual practice yourself. You may then connect with the Fabric and know for yourself that the Truths represented here are presented accurately, properly, with no compromise, and with no strings attached.

Before jumping into the contents of this book, a few final comments are in order. First of all, if you haven't read the previous books in the *Lightning Path* series, i.e. *The Rocket Scientists' Guide to Authentic Spirituality, The Great Awakening: Concepts and Techniques for Successful Spiritual Practice,* and *The Lightning Path Core Lesson Book,* I suggest you do that before proceeding. *The Rocket Scientists' Guide, The Great Awakening,* and the *Core Lesson Booklet* provide concepts, ideas, and practices that will help you get the most out of this treatise. In other words, this book *builds* from the previous books, and although you can get a lot out of this book without reading the other Lightning Path core books, especially if you have a previous amateur or professional interest in mysticism, I believe you'll get much more out of this book if you do the practical work as well.[9]

Speaking of reading the other books at this level, I should probably say at this point that my writing tends to be iterative. That is, you can read this book now but then, after reading several of the other books on the Lightning Path, come back to this book and get even more out of it. The reason for that is that all my books are written with a practical focus and that is to remove the Blindfold (see my Parable of the Blindfold) that prevents connection to Fabric of Consciousness and access to internal noesis. There is nothing particularly mystical or magical about the blindfold. The blindfold is rooted in "old energy" ideas and concepts, and our violent and toxic, class based socialization process. The process of removing the blindfold is a process of healing the physical unit (body, but mostly mind), establishing right thought, right action, and right environment, and nurturing the full range of emotional, intellectual, and intuitive faculties. What I am trying to say here is simple. Your appreciation of this book will be enhanced if you are also in the process of "removing the Blindfold".

In the context of removing the Blindfold I should say that there is a bit of work involved. Removing the blindfold and destroying The System is complicated. The reality is that we are all deeply embedded in the muck and mud of illusion and

---

[9] The most inexpensive way to acquire all four books at the Lightning Path Core level of study is as an eBook or print package, available from the Lightning Path store

http://www.thelightningpath.com/product/lightning-path-core-study-package/

delusion (maya in some traditions) and it takes, in addition to time and commitment from you, a carefully constructed "bridge" to get us out of the muck of delusion and back into the full light of our collective divinity. This path you are on, this Lightning Path, is iterative because this bridge that is being built here is not an exclusively linear, left-brain bridge (if it were it simply would not be effective). This bridge is constructed with words, images, and metaphors, in a sort of spiral of enlightenment that gets you out of the "valley of the shadow of death" and into the full light of God (with a big "G") and Spirit. To get the most out of this path, to "traverse the bridge" so to speak, you have to go back and forth as you slowly eject all the old world dogma and deception from your consciousness and replace it with the shining capital "T" Truths of God, god, and Spirit. The advice here is simple: Expect to come back to the materials more than once. I know we are all pressed for time these days, but you will often find you get a lot more out of a book like this one the second, third, or even fourth time you go through it.

Second, depending on where you are coming from, this book may represent quite a revolution for you. Indeed, if you are just freeing yourself from a dogmatic religious or scientific background the spirituality represented in this book may represent a total reversal in your understanding of creation. In fact, you may find a lot of what you feel are "standard and accepted" exoteric and esoteric spiritual truths either totally absent or completely reversed by the material in this book. For example, in the conception of creation outlined in this book, there is no room for hell, no conception of spiritual "evolution," no notion of hierarchy, no allowance for "evil," no justification for suffering and pain, and no excuses to let you off the hook. In fact, those who are paying close attention will find me working very hard to erase and revise much of the standard dogmatic spiritual prescriptions for understanding existence. If you do find yourself taken aback by the extent of the revision, take a deep breath. I'm sure you'll find, if you are open, and if you ask God, your guides, or the angels for confirmation, that the universe will provide you with the confirmation you need to have the faith required to at least consider the truth of what I am telling you.

Third, this book is written with different, how shall we say, intellectual temperatures. The preface to this series, and to a lesser extent the preface to this volume, has a strong scholarly flavor. By contrast the revelatory sections of this text are more open and transparent. The difference in temperature is a function of the difference of intent and goal. My goal in the prefaces is intellectual contextualization and theoretical exploration. My goal in the revelatory parts of this text are transparency and clarity of presentation. In the revelatory sections of this text I aim to make high level mystical revelations available to everyone over the age of nineteen,[10] and the language and presentation reflects this. You may be initially uncomfortable with the shift in temperature, and even uncomfortable with the style of writing in the revelatory sections. If so, be patient and bear with me because you may feel there are rough spots. While I would not want to push *ineffability* as a necessary feature of mystical revelation, I

---

[10] I haven't forgotten the children. Prior to that, Truths represented here presented to children in my children's books, Captain Tristan and I, Vayda Jayne Bean, and future efforts.

would say that finding the words and ways to express mystical experience, especially in a generic, "all-access" sort of way, is a challenge.

Fourth, I would recommend that past this preface you approach the revelatory sections of this text from a mystical perspective. In line with research suggestive that mystical and paranormal phenomenon are features of a healthy right brain hemisphere (Roll & Williams, 2010), and in line with my own spiritual guidance that stipulates deep breathing, relaxed mental states, firm intent, and development of the right brain through music, art, and music are essential pre-requisites for authentic and healthy mystical experience (Sharp, 2007, 2103a), I would not recommend jumping into the revelatory sections of this book immediately upon completing the prefaces. Reading the prefaces, reading a scholarly journal, or doing other sorts of "left-brain" dominant activities activates the left-brain and puts you in a space not conducive to "mystical awareness". If you are going to get the most out of this book you need to shift cognitive processes over to the right side. You can do that by engaging in forms of meditation that quiet the chatty left brain, by going on a nature walk, by engaging a state of mindfulness, by smoking a small amount of marijuana, by praying for guidance and enlightenment, etc. Many techniques for shifting consciousness are available to you. You don't have to shift a lot, at least initially, but you do have to shift. If you jump right in while the left brain is active and buzzing you will be wasting your time since the words on the page will be nothing more than words on the page.

Fifth, finally, and much to the chagrin and perhaps annoyance of someone with a standard background in

English, this book is not written from a consistent perspective. That is, I shift points of view around throughout the text, not a lot, but enough to make people who think that I should remain locked in a single perspective (e.g., abstract and impersonal third person) uncomfortable. For example, I start off "in the beginning" from the perspective of the original monadic spark of consciousness or "I" (i.e., it is god with a little "g" who is talking in the first few pages), move on to the perspective of "we" and then rock back and forth between "I," "you," "me," and "we" in a loose and fluid sort of way. This rocking may cause a little nausea in some, and if so I ask your indulgence. The reason I do this is because we (and by "we" I mean all incarnated sparks of consciousness) are simply not locked into a single perspective. Because of the nature of The Fabric of Consciousness we can, if we are open and connected, "see" and understand things from multiple perspectives. In the interests of clarity and ease of explanation, it just makes sense to present information from the most relevant perspective. In the beginning, that would be the perspective of god with a little "g," but later on it would be the perspective of others. By the end of the book I believe you will understand this clearly and hopefully have become comfortable with all the "shifts in perspective" that I tend to make throughout this book. If not, my apologies.

In any case, that's enough chit-chat. Now it is time to begin, and begin we shall. Following a brief mystically oriented introduction we shall initiate volume one of the *Book of Light* series where all good accounts of creation must begin and that is, in the beginning....

Introduction

Greetings and welcome to Volume One of The Book of Light. The book that you now have in your hand is my take on answering the really big spiritual and philosophical questions[11] that we, as earthlings, may have had at one time or another. These big questions are the important questions of our existence, questions like "What is the nature of God?" "What is the nature of creation?" "What is my (your/our) purpose?" and more. Indeed, everything from the essence of creation, the path of the Unfolding, the dimensional levels of creation, and even your relationship with God and creation will be covered in this book. If I do my job with any degree of success, by the end of this four-volume set you will have a whole new perspective on things of a spiritual nature and, more importantly, you will have a whole new perspective on where you fit into the general scheme of things. Indeed, depending on how far you've already come, reading these books could be quite the revolution, even revelation, for you.

Before getting too far into this book, I should warn you in advance that you will not find certain aspects of standard "old energy" spiritual answers to the big questions in this book. There is, in short, no church canon or scientific scripture here and so for some of you this book may represent a fundamental intellectual, psychological, and even emotional challenge as you are asked to reevaluate your taken-for-granted answers. For example, I am not going to regurgitate

---

[11] See http://www.thespiritwiki.com/index.php/Big_Questions

old and oh-so-boring "truths" about the fall of humanity or the descent of the apes. I am not going to tell you stories that justify judgment and punishment, or that bind you to endless karmic work on The Wheel.[12] I am not going to threaten you with tales of hell and damnation, or karmic retribution, if you fail to follow the rules. I'm also not going to excuse pain, suffering, greed, graft, corruption, and violence. I am going to provide no justifications for the obscene way in which some people have billions of dollars while others (most notably children) die every second of every day of every year of every decade from poverty, malnutrition, and starvation. Any notion that obscene wealth is a function of Darwinian mechanisms of survival, any belief that we choose to be born into poverty and woe, any hypothesis that posits great evil as a justification for mass violence, is poppycock. I am also going to condemn violence of any kind, whether that be physical, emotional, psychological, or spiritual. It is never OK to hurt another person, period. Violence of any kind (including "holy wars," Crusades, Jihad's, emotional abuse, psychological attacks) and for whatever reason (i.e. they "deserve" it, they are "evil", they are primitive animals, etc.) is off the spiritual table. The truth is, there are no valid excuses for violence. Any idea that justifies or excuses pain, suffering, greed, graft, corruption, and violence is ideology. Any idea that says pain builds character is a bald-faced lie. Any perspective that says it is OK to kill people because they are evil is spiritual bullshit. In short, many of the answers, stated outright or

---

[12] http://www.thespiritwiki.com/index.php/The_Wheel

implied, that you may currently have to the "big questions" are hereby and summarily erased from further consideration.

I suppose the question at this point is, if I am going to summarily dismiss many of the standard and dogmatic answers to the big questions that you may have, what am I going to replace those with? Without getting into any detail up front, let me just say here that I am going to replace all the old dogmatic answers that you may have with the high Truth of our origin, identity, and purpose. Starting from "the beginning" in this volume one, walking through the unfolding of physical creation in volumes two and three, and concluding with an overview of our current reality in volume four, I am going to tell you the truth about who you are, where you came from, and why you are here. I am going to walk you through the hallways of creation and I am going to show you the truth of your divinity from "the beginning." To be as blunt as possible, I am going to show you that you are God/Consciousness/Light, and I am going to elaborate on the physical, cosmological, and theological implications of this fundamental spiritual Truth.[13] After I'm done here, it will be your choice what you want to do with the information. You

---

[13] As you will see as you wend your way through the Lightning Path, the implications of the fundamental spiritual Truth discussed in this Book of Light are profound. In this book we'll deal only with the physical, cosmological, and theological implications. Elsewhere on the Lightning Path we will examine the economic, sociological, and even psychological implications of rooting identity, reality, and experience in consciousness.

can, if you so wish, go back to living your life the way you have always lived your life, bound to the work-a-day wheel and remaining silent and sheepish out of fear or misconception or, my personal choice, you can embrace your divinity, awaken and activate, take responsibility for the nonsense in your life and on this earth, and start changing things for the better. It is within your power, but it is your choice.

Of course, I realize you may or may not be interested in this. You may have come here for the same reasons you have come to previous spiritual texts. You may have come because you wanted me to say that things are okay with you and this earth and that you can go on in the same fashion you've always gone. But let's face it, things are not okay. From a political, social, psychological, spiritual, and environmental point of view, things are bad and no amount of fancy Hollywood production or sophisticated self-denial can deny this truth anymore. Face it or not, take it or leave it, it is your choice. But do not kid yourself. You will live with the consequences of your choice. Just don't expect others to live in that old world nonsense with you. We are tired of it.

To those of you still reading, I say welcome! I believe those who remain here fall into two basic categories of readers. The first group drawn to this book and still reading at this point will be those individuals unfamiliar with my writings but who nevertheless have an interest in things of an esoteric or deep spiritual nature. You may be new on "the path" or have been searching for a while. You may have stumbled onto this book or have been led here by a friend but whatever reason you came, however long you've been searching, it doesn't matter. To all of you seekers of truth I say again welcome. My name is Michael Sharp, and this is the way I see the universe.

Speaking of the way I see things, I will tell you up front that my way of seeing the universe is probably not like the way you are used to seeing it. This will be especially true if you have any previous spiritual training in some sort of organized religious setting (e.g., Catholic, Masonic, Buddhist, etc.). To be frank, my universe is totally different from those universes. In my universe there is no evil, there is only the light of God. In my universe there is no hierarchy, there is only the Truth of our shared Divinity. In my universe there is no required poverty, there is only the divine reality of universal abundance. In my universe there is no "karma" (at least as typically understood as punitive cosmic "justice"), there is only our divine and collective responsibility. As you can see, I don't share many of the standard beliefs. I do not believe, for example, in Darwin (and although I am convinced of evolution, I do not worship it as many do), I do not believe in Satan (though I do understand people do bad things), I do not believe in perdition (except of our own making), and I do not believe in sin. I do not believe life is supposed to be a struggle to survive, I do not believe that some people deserve to starve, and I do not believe that weakness is an excuse for deprivation. In fact, I believe we all issue from the same source, that we all create the world and the universe, that we all part of the same glorious *Fabric of Consciousness,*[14] and that we are thus all equal in the *eyes of God.* Because of this, because we are all one, I believe there is no excuse for suffering, poverty, war, and violence. As the Source of all things I believe we (you/I/we) are Divine, and if something is wrong on this world, not only is it our responsibility to change it, but we are in fact the only ones who can change it because we are the front line workers in this creative drama and if we do not do it, it does not get done.

Now, I understand this may be a lot to swallow. For some reading this, this may be heresy, blasphemy even. Thankfully, however, this is not the Middle Ages and nobody will be burned for merely uttering a heresy or a blasphemy, so do not worry. If you have difficulty with what I'm saying, if you dislike what you find here but find you simply must read through anyway, just view the truths in this book as my way of seeing things and leave it at that. After all, it is your choice what to believe. I am not here to convert you or preach at you, I am not here to save you or judge you, I am just here to provide an alternative to the old world spirituality[15] that we have been forced to consume for so many centuries. Take it or leave it, now, later, or never, it is up to you. There is no implied threat (i.e., you will not burn in hell if you make the "wrong" choice) and there will be no skin off my back, this time. If you want to believe you are a descended ape, if you

---

[14] See www.thespiritwiki.com/index.php/Fabric_of_Consciousness

[15] See www.thespiritwiki.com/index.php/Old_World_Spirituality.

want to embrace your original sin as rejects from The Garden, if you want to believe in evil, if you want to justify suffering and abuse, if you want to see the universe as necessarily violent, hostile, and chaotic, if you want to listen to the priests and the Pharisees and the gurus who tell you that you are less than who you truly are, feel free! Believe what you want, do what you want, it is up to you. It won't change the course of history now unfolding, and it won't change who you truly are deep down inside.

The second group of people drawn to this book and still reading at this point will be those already familiar with my writings. You know who you are. You are the people who have already stepped onto the Lightning Path and have come here looking for more. You have read the preliminary materials, done some preliminary work, and now you are ready to move a step further on the path. In the vernacular of the new age movement, you are here to raise your vibration, ascend your body, and move forward into a more light-filled and eternal sort of existence. To you folks I also say welcome! This book you have in your hands is indeed the next step (or at least one of the steps) in the core level of study. In this four-volume set you will find all the information you need in order to properly orient your bodily consciousness (i.e., your brain's mind) towards either descent of the light (i.e., descent of the holy spirit, birth of Christ consciousness, expansion of consciousness into the body, or whatever you want to call it)

and/or ascent of the body into higher consciousness. It really doesn't matter which way you look at it; either way it's the same deal.

This next step in your core level of study is relatively easy. What you basically have to accomplish at this point is a simple shift in perspective. Stop thinking you are your body and instead start identifying with your true self, your higher consciousness. It is easy to state the nature of this shift. Understand that you are consciousness, pure and simple. Understand that your body is a vehicle for your consciousness and nothing more. You are not male, you are not female, you are not black, you are not white, you are not even human. Your container is, your body is, but you are not. At this point, you need to shift out of identification with your vehicle and identify instead with the consciousness that animates you. In order to facilitate this shift, in this book I am going to discuss the nature of consciousness, remind you of your divinity, and give you a tool to help you make the shift in perspective. The tool amounts to hope and a prayer. Hope, or rather faith (at least in the early stages) that all this spiritual stuff is true and a prayer (see appendix) that helps guide your body into a new perspective and full realization of its divinity. Hopefully this will be enough to facilitate a shift in perspective for you. It's not that hard.

As a side benefit to the work we do here, I am also going to start the process of inoculating you against all that viciously implanted propaganda that teaches you the lie that you are "less than" in every way. You might know what I am talking about here, and if not you will certainly know by the end of the LP Intermediate level of study. **The propaganda of**

"less than" is that constellation of ideas and ideology (found everywhere from science to religion, popular philosophy to "secret" doctrine) that says you are a broken, inferior, cast out reject of God or nature. If you want to go any further on this path, you are going to have to stop thinking like that. You will have to stop believing you are "less than" anything and start thinking you are equal to everything. It's that simple. This book, along with the LP Intermediate level materials, *The Book of the Triumph of Spirit* and *The Book of the Triumph of Spirit Master Key*, will help you with that. It will help you remove all the "wrong thinking" that has been put into your head in order to limit you and keep you disconnected and impotent, and it will provide you with "right thinking"[16] (i.e. concepts and ideas and archetypes) that does not limit you but that encourages and supports the *full manifestation of your divinity through your physical unit.* I know it may not seem like much now, but establishing right thought will make a huge difference in not only how you see yourself and this world, your state of emotional, mental, and even physical health, but how you interact, move, and manifest within it.

Now I know I say this won't be difficult but I cannot kid you here: There is a bit of work. If you want to move forward from here you are going to have to get over all those nonsense beliefs (i.e. all that wrong thinking) imposed on you since your birth here on Earth. That can be quite a challenge, for a

---

[16] See http://www.thespiritwiki.com/index.php/Right_Thought for a definition of Right Thinking.

couple of reasons. One, there are a lot of ideas to get rid of and two (and as we will see when we tackle planetary archetypes at the LP Intermediate level of study) the ideas themselves are deviously crafted and deeply ingrained. As a result, you are going to have to work at it. You will, in short, have to reprogram your consciousness. That will take some time and effort, and this book and the prayer (included at the back) is only the start of it. You start by meditating/praying (see appendix) with The Prayer for a few minutes in the morning, noon, and at night. Once you are done here, once you have a good sense that you are immortal consciousness and not dirt and dust, the real work of archetypal analysis and reprogramming begins. It is important you do this. If there is one lesson that you should take away from reading this book it is this: *Consciousness is the root of all things* or, as I also like to say:

> As Above in Consciousness,
> So Below in Matter

Put another way, the ideas that we have in our brains pretty much determine the reality that manifests around us.[17] This works at a collective level to be sure (it is why so much money and effort is put into controlling the ideas of this planet), but

---

[17] Determines within the parameters of the qualities, dimensions, sephiroth of creation, qualities that provide some basic conditions within which our creative endeavors unfold. You'll learn all about the qualities/dimensions/sephiroth of creation in the course of this four volume Book of Light.

it also works at an individual level, with your own ideas about who you are, where you came from, and what you are doing here. If you believe you are a karmic reject, a descended ape, or a broken-down angel, then this is what you become. On the other hand if you (if we all) can come to believe the Truth, that you are an immortal spark of consciousness, an equal part of the great Fabric of Consciousness, or God with a little "g" as I like to say, then this is what you (what we) will shortly become.

Of course in the end the choice is yours. You can continue to believe in the nonsense ideology of "less than," and (rich or poor) live out the rest of your days in quiet pain and increasing desperation, or you can finally put the nonsense behind you, step onto this path, embrace your Divinity, and begin the journey home. Step forward, embrace your divinity, and return or stay locked in the ideology of less than. The choice is yours.

Part One
The Nature of God

I AM Pure Awareness, the Fire of Consciousness

In the beginning, there was only consciousness.

In the beginning, there was only awareness.

In the beginning, there was only "I."

In the beginning, there was only a single speck of light, a single *perspective* of self, and a single monadic spark.

In some esoteric writing this initial state of "I" is conceptualized by a period or a point. This is accurate and useful. The point has **no dimensions**, no experience of time or space, no beginning, and no end.

The point is pure awareness, plain and simple!

This is the Truth.

This is the original nature of "I."

In the beginning I AM pure awareness.

In the beginning I AM pure light.

In the beginning I AM the pure fire of consciousness.

I AM Alpha and Omega

And now you know the first and most important Truth of consciousness. I AM pure awareness, pure light. And I AM more than this.

I AM everything and nothing.

I AM a forever of new beginnings.

I AM Alpha and Omega.

I AM beginning without end.

I AM eternity.

How could it be otherwise?

In the beginning there was only "ME."

In between there is only "ME."

In the end there will be only "ME."

Indeed, there will never be a time or a place or a space where "I" do not exist for I AM eternity, Alpha and Omega, beginning without end.

I AM Bliss, Love, and Compassion

And now you know two of the core Truths of creation. I AM pure awareness, the fire of consciousness, and I am the alpha and the omega, the beginning without end. But I AM more than this.

I AM also pure bliss, pure joy, and loving compassion.

I AM the original cosmic smiley face.

How could it be otherwise?

Being the light of all creation and the Alpha and Omega, being everything and no-thing beginning without end is an awesome thing to be. There is nothing more wondrous and grand than this and my ongoing awareness of this truth brings me unmitigated bliss, love, and joy. I'm happy with myself, I love myself, and will love all the things that issue from me.

In Truth I AM pure ecstasy, I AM bliss eternal, I AM Love without end.

I AM the Seed

And now you know three of the core Truths of unity and oneness. I AM pure awareness, the Fire of consciousness, I AM the Alpha and the Omega, the beginning without end, and I AM joy, bliss, and love eternal. But I AM much more than this.

I AM also the pure potential of manifestation.

I AM the ultimate and only source of all things.

I AM the seed from which all creation grows.

How could it be otherwise?

I AM awareness pure and simple, I AM everything and nothing, I AM the light of all creation, I AM Alpha and Omega. Nothing exists beside me, nothing exists in front of me, and nothing exists without me. Only I exist, only I can exist, and so all things must exist within me.

Truly I AM the Seed of all Creation

I AM Powerful Without Limit

And now you know four of the core truths of creation. I AM pure awareness, the Fire of consciousness, I AM the Alpha and the Omega, the beginning without end, I AM joy and bliss eternal, and I AM the Seed from which all creation flows

But I AM more than all these.

I AM also without limit, and without boundary.

I AM the limitless potential of imagination.

How could it be otherwise?

I AM consciousness pure and simple and you cannot limit consciousness.

How can you limit thought?

How can you limit ideas?

How can you limit imagination?

The truth is, you cannot. It is impossible to limit ideas, it is impossible to restrict imagination, and therefore no boundaries exist around MY light. Consciousness is a dream and you cannot limit a dream.

I may dream anything I want.

I may think all things.

I AM The Limitless Potential of Imagination.

I AM the omnipotent power of creation.

The Limit of My Experience

And now you know *the Foundation of Divinity*. I AM pure awareness, the Fire of consciousness, I AM the Alpha and the Omega, the beginning without end, I AM joy, bliss, and love eternal, and I AM without limit and boundary. And in all of this, I AM, for the most part, satisfied. However, there is one tiny problem. There is one wrinkle that emerges and causes consternation and that wrinkle is in the limitation of imagination.[18]

Now, I know I said that my imagination is without limit and that I can think anything I want without boundary, and that is true. I can think and imagine anything I want. Nothing limits me, nevertheless I AM limited. Know however that limitation is not an arbitrarily imposed external limitation. The problem is internal. The limitation of my imagination is caused by the limitation of my experience. You see, consciousness is dynamic and changes with *experience*. It grows and expands, it interacts, and it develops only through experience. However, consciousness is a fire and without the **air of inspiration** that comes from *challenge* and new experience, without *fuel* for the fire, the fire dwindles. And when the fire dwindles, imagination expires and no new thoughts are thought.

And it does happen.

In the beginning, when there was only me, myself, and I, and when nothing existed except the pure awareness, bliss, and potential of consciousness, *imagination was limited.* No matter how grand and wonderful I might have been in my blissful point-edness, there were only so many new thoughts I could think about. Eventually, inevitably, "it" would happen and I would run out of things to think about. And when that

---

[18] For the sake of technical clarity we shall define imagination as the aspect of consciousness that has the ability to think new thoughts.

inevitably happened, when I ran out of new things to think about, I experienced the only experience that consciousness may experience when it runs out of things to think about and that was excruciatingly, painful B.O.R.E.D.O.M. With no new thoughts to think, with all things having run their course in consciousness, boredom was the only outcome. And the longer this went on, the longer there were no new thoughts, the longer I had no experience to fuel the fire of my imagination, the more painful the boredom became. And because I despised the experience of boredom, and because I hated the experience of pain, I could not let it go on. **I had to rise to the challenge**! I had to do something. I had to find an experience (or experiences) that would provide inspiration, fan the fires of consciousness, and make my imagination soar. If I could not find something to ease the excruciating pain of boredom, then respite would only come by descending back into the oblivion of unconscious sleep (see volume two). But the bliss and joy of awareness was wonderful and so the thought of returning did not appeal. Still, it was a problem. Since I AM the Alpha and Omega of creation, since nothing existed but that which exists within the consciousness of I, what could there be that would provide the experience that would fan the fires and alleviate the pain?

Part Two
The Nature of Creation

Row Row Row Your Boat...

I agree, it was a bit of a quandary.

What happens when I run out of things to think about?

I AM Alpha and Omega!

I AM beginning without end!

Only I exist!

What happens when even my own bellybutton disgusts me?

What happens when I get tired of I?

It's a philosophical conundrum, I agree, but "I" wasn't that worried. After all, I had an eternity to think, and I had no doubt whatsoever that somewhere in the Unfolding of eternity I'd figure something out. It was necessary and inevitable, for in the *Unfolding* of eternity, no problem ever goes unsolved. All I needed was a little patience, and so I thought and thought and pondered the problem and as I thought and pondered *inspiration* eventually came and danced gently, like a brush of *air*, over the *fire* of my consciousness. And as the inspiration blew, the flames danced higher and a new idea was born.

From the forge of consciousness a solution had emerged!

And so I said to myself, with conviction and authority:

> I AM THE FIRE of Consciousness,
> I AM THE AIR of my Inspiration,
> and what I need is a new Toy.

Now you have to admit, it was a perfect idea, and a brilliant way forward.

What other solution was there?

I could either create a new toy or continue in a downward spiraling solipsistic circle of ennui and frankly, the thought of that spiral into monotony was unbearable. Therefore, a new toy was the solution.

A new toy would add interest.

A new toy would add variety.

A new toy would allow me to play, and in that play I would experience, and from that experience I would be able to think new thoughts. It was an exciting idea, and as I thought about it I realized I wanted to do it right. After all, I didn't want to create just any toy. I didn't want a mere lump of mud, for example, or a blob of clay. I didn't want to turn around in boredom after only a few moments and have to do it all again. I wanted to create something that would hold my attention for more than a fleeting instant. But what toy would satisfy something as magnificent as pure, powerful, eternal, consciousness? It was a bit of a conundrum to be sure; but I wasn't worried. Eternity is a long time, after all, and in the Unfolding of eternity, no conundrum goes unsolved. And so, after only a little thought, inspiration blew, the fires crackled, and a new idea was born. For my new toy, I would create the energetic equivalent of silly putty.

I would manufacture the Plasticine[19] of Paradise.

I would serve up the Waters of Creation.

Now don't laugh!

It was a brilliant idea and the perfect solution. This new energy of creation, this Plasticine of Paradise, would be the ideal building block for creative play. It would have to be, because I would make it ideal. It would be "my thing" after all, and being my thing I would be able to make it anything I wanted, and so that is what I did. I created the energy of creation (a.k.a. the Waters of Creation or the Plasticine of Paradise) and I gave it features that would make it the ideal foil for my creative endeavor.

First of all, I made it totally flexible. I knew right away and without any thought that if *the energy* (or the water) was going to prevent boredom, *the energy* (or the water) would have to be flexible.

There could be no limitation on form.

---

[19] Plasticine is a registered trademark of Flair Leisure Products, plc.

There could be no restriction in function.

The energy would have to be multi-purpose. It would have to be capable of doing many things. The energy would be capable of doing everything and being anything that I wanted it to be! A single solitary form, for example, or a hard block of stone (or clay or mud) that I had to chip away at with lots of effort would make no sense at all. Without easy flexibility, without malleability, the toy would be no better than a lump of stone–fun for a bit, but getting boring quite quickly. Therefore, and clearly, the first characteristic of The Waters would have to be total flexibility. This was important if boredom was to be averted, and so I thought it would be best to make a "law" out of this feature. Not a *real* law of the type that you must follow or else, but a sort of creative guideline that would remind me (and later we) of this critical creative principle.[20] I would call this "law" the First Law of Creation,

---

[20] I would like to take a moment to put to rest any notion that there is ever anything like a *law* of creation that we must follow or that binds our creative endeavors (the "law of attraction" pops to mind here). Laws like that are dreamed up by sleepy humans disconnected from The Fabric of Consciousness and are not part of the Truth of creation. Creation is obviously not like that. How could it be? Creation, because it starts as a dream in the mind of "I," and continues as a result of the fiery emanation of consciousness, has absolutely no limitation other than the limit on imagination already pointed out. You can basically dream, or think, whatever you want. You are limited only by the limits of your imagination (which are in turn limited by the experiences you have had). Any "laws" that "I" may have come up with are nothing more than creative guidelines

and it would read...

The First Law - Flexible

The energy of creation shall have no limitation[21]

The energy of creation would provide absolute flexibility as a primary and standard feature.

Gently Down the Stream

Now, once I had settled on absolute flexibility as the primary feature of the energy of creation, the next question was how would I work and play with this energy?

After all, being merely a spark of consciousness (albeit a very bright one), being only a glob of infinite light, I had no hands and no arms, no feet and no toes so, how would I play?

---

that we (and by "we" I mean Immortal Spirit) agree upon before beginning the creative process. Of course these laws have creative consequences which may later constrain creation. That is, a decision made at one point may provide parameters that *must* be followed later on. For example, if you are building a cabinet and you choose to use oak wood rather than, for example, fiber board, then this choice will constrain you in certain ways later on. But this isn't the same thing as saying that there is an absolute law that governs your creative choices. It is all open to modification.

[21] Salicadoola.

How would I make it do the things I wanted it to do?

A quandary?

Yes!

Unsolvable?

No!

With an eternity of eternities to ponder, no problem goes unsolved and so eventually inspiration would blow, the fires would dance and an idea would be born. It was necessary, it was inevitable, and that is exactly what happened. After a certain amount of time had passed, I realized that if I was pure consciousness, the energy of creation would have to respond to that consciousness.

It would have to dance to ideas.

It would have to respond to mind!

There was no other choice.

The Waters would have to respond to contemplative intent.

There was no other way.

The Waters would fill my imagination or reduce to a single speck based on the simple direction of thought. The Waters would be a kind of cosmic mind mush that would follow, in *reflective* fashion, the thought of the creator. And once again this seemed important enough to set into "law" and so that is what I did. I made a second law and the law read...

> Energy follows intent
>
> or
>
> Where thought doth go,
> energy doth follow
>
> or
>
> As above in consciousness, so below in matter22

I could find a lot of ways to express this law, but they would all mean exactly the same—the Waters of Creation would respond, and correspond, to the thought of the creator, that's me. The Waters, in short, would be reflective.

Merrily, Merrily, Merrily, Merrily...

Pausing to consider I think you will agree, the potential here is exciting. A new toy that does anything you want and becomes anything you want according to every thought in your magnificent creator mind is magnificent! Still, and although the idea was magnificent, one last little detail, one tiny little hiccup that might prevent the manifestation of this wonderful new plaything, remained. To understand this problem we have to go a little deeper and ask the basic question "How does a single point of consciousness, the

---

[22] Menchicaboola.

supreme awareness of 'I,' the Alpha and Omega, the beginning without end, and the only thing that can ever exist, create something (anything, in fact) outside of I?"

That is, if only I exist, where will the energy come from, where will it go, and where will it exist?

It is a critical question!

Remember, I AM Alpha and Omega, I AM beginning without end, and nothing exists outside of me.

I AM *all that* I AM so where will the energy be?

It is a poser, I agree, but once again not an unsolvable one. A bit of patience, a little thought, a bit of inspiration and *poof*, the elegant and inevitable answer arrived. To enable the instantiation of energy, to create the Plasticine of paradise, The Waters of Creation would exist as a dream inside the mind of I (a dream inside the mind of God).

Life is but a Dream

Now, I am sure you will agree, this was the perfect solution and obviously the only way forward. What other choice was there? If only I exist, if nothing exists outside of me, then everything (and I do mean everything) has to be, in one way or another, a part of consciousness, including the energy of creation!

The Waters must be a part of I.

There is no other way.

After all, only I exist.

I AM the Alpha and the Omega.

I AM the beginning without end.

I AM the fire of consciousness.

I AM the air of inspiration

I AM the water of creation.

I AM all things and at this point in the Unfolding, at the cusp of the birth of creation, I AM bursting at the seams with excitement.

Now, I realize that at this point almost all of you are thinking that we have come to the point of "the big bang," when light exploded in creation and the universe as we (and by "we" I mean those of us incarnated in a physical body *inside* the waters of creation) know it was born. Unfortunately, however, we have not arrived at the point of the big bang. That as yet comes later. At our current point in the discussion of the unfolding of creation, that is, at the point where The Waters come into existence as a dream inside the mind of I, there was nothing big or flashy about it at all.

The dawn of creation was simply not like that.

Indeed, the Waters came into existence with more of a shudder (of the kind that runs zipping up and down your spine) than anything else.

Consciousness is like a great ocean. It is fluid, constant, and flowing. When thought emerges from consciousness, it is like a wave emerging from the sea.

This is how The Waters of Creation emerged.

Like a wave emerging from the still point of consciousness the Waters of Creation gained reality as I (and by "I" I mean god with a little "g") thought about it.

The more I considered it, the more it was real.

The more I understand what its features would be, the more it came into existence.

Put another way, as I *named it, it became.* When the thought was complete, when the idea was fully formed, the Word (of God) was made flesh and The Waters of Creation were born.

No separation.

No distinction.

No break in the flow.

Thought is creation/creation is thought.

This is the nature of creation.

This is the nature of The Water.

Before we move on, a couple of additional comments are in order. First of all, let us recall the first two "laws" of creation, *energy is without limit* and *energy follows intent.* A bit of clarification is now in order here.

I know that earlier I said that these laws were not laws but reminders of features that I gave the energy in the beginning. While this is, for the most part, true, it is not the whole story. I do have the laws as reminders, but the energy works the way it does because of its nature, and not because of any divine decree.

That is, it wasn't really my decision in the beginning that gave the energy its characteristic features. Energy is *the way it is* (i.e., without limit and always following the intent of consciousness) because of *what it is*, a dream inside the mind of I. As such, the Waters of Creation, the dream inside the mind of "I" can only ever be an exact replica of what is in consciousness.

I know I'm being a bit repetitive here, but this bears repeating. The Water is Consciousness/Consciousness is the Water and The Water acts the way it does because of what it is, a dreamlike reflection in the mind of I.

Make sure this is clear to you.

The Waters are without limit because consciousness is without limit.

The Waters respond to consciousness because The Water is a thought within consciousness.

It is the way it is because that is the way it is.

I know this is repetitive, but there is a good reason to emphasize this. These are important features of creation and understanding (and remembering!) them is critical if we want to be effective creators. The bottom line is, we must get it right in consciousness before we get it right in reality!

As above in consciousness,
So below in matter

The truth is, if we (and by "we" I mean the bright lights of consciousness incarnated in the human physical unit) have a lot of misconceptions about the way creation works or what it is all about, if we have a lot of fear and anger, if we have a lot of erroneous ideas about what creation should be, we could end up with a broken-down, run-down, dilapidated creation.

And it could be worse than even that!

The truth is, if we don't know the Truth, if we don't understand that consciousness is and always will be the source, if we buy into the dogmatic lies, we could end up powerless, impotent, and subject to somebody else's creative whims, and we don't want that. So remember, the Waters of Creation are always a reflection of the contents and ideas in consciousness.[23]

---

[23] All this talk about "laws" and "not laws" isn't to say that the rules can't be changed; they can be and all it takes to accomplish that is general agreement from all participating parties. It is certainly true that *energy is without limitation* (the first law) and *energy follows intent* (the second law), but these laws can be changed simply by adjusting the way we think about The Waters. For example, if we are taught that we are limited and powerless (as many of the old world spiritualities teach us), and if we accept this, then this *breaks* the laws of creation as we become that which we think we are (i.e. limited and impotent). Put the right ideas into someone's head, i.e. make them think they are broken angels or karmic rejects, make them think they are struggling to "evolve," and this is exactly what they

Now that you are clear about the nature of energy, which is like a reflection of the mind of God (or god), within the mind of God, we can introduce a third "law" that, like the other two, is spoken as a reminder but exists because of the nature of the Water and that law is simply this:

The Third Law - Responsive

Energy responds to intent instantly and literally[24]

This basically means that whatever I think will be manifest instantly and literally in creation. That is, there will be no delay between thought and manifestation. The Waters will, in short, be responsive! Of course, the same comments about laws and rules mentioned in footnote 23 apply here. This law arises because of the nature of the Waters as a dream inside

---

become, broken, rejected, unevolved, and powerless.

Now if you are paying attention you should begin to realize just how important our ideas about ourselves really are. Indeed, how you think about God, creation, and your place in it is absolutely critical. If you have the wrong ideas about things you will be diminished in your power and potential. The truth is, you will always be exactly what you think you are. If you choose to believe the limiting ideas of old energy spirituality, if you choose to limit yourself with ideas and archetypes about your own FOOLish nature then all I can say is Bippity, Boppitty, Boo your wish will come true.

[24] Bippity Boppity Boo!

65

the mind of I and not because of any desire or decree on the part of some executive authority. If I have a thought, it is instantly reflected in the Water because of what the Water is, mere reflection of the mind of God (or god). There is no other way for creation to unfold. It is simply the nature of I.

Pause for a moment and reflect upon these three laws. Consider these three laws *The Foundation of Creation*. They are the important creative principles that you <u>must</u> remember if you want to dance like the master of creation that you are, so remind yourself daily. These laws are the foundation for all your creative work.[25]

---

[25] I do not want to leave anyone with the impression that just because creation emerges from energy and just because energy is merely a thought in the mind of God that creation is thus somehow wispy and insubstantial. The dream of creation in the mind of God, the Word of God, is not like the limited and vaporous dream of the physical brain. The dreams of Spirit are far more potent and viable than the dreams as expressed by the physical neuron. In fact, the consciousness of Spirit is so powerful and so bright that the dreams of Spirit take on all the reality and depth that Spirit intends in them. In the end (and in the beginning) you cannot separate one from the other. The dream is as real as the consciousness that dreams it. And believe me when I tell you, *God is real.* I know that some of you will have trouble with the idea of the primacy of consciousness. Stick with it and remember this truth. **The only *real* thing in this universe is the consciousness of God**. Explore this novel idea awhile and soon you may ponder how you could have ever believed that this world had any power or authority over you at all!

And so, there you have it.

And so, there I was.

And so, with energy in mind I got down to the serious business of play, and let me tell you I had fun!

As I turned my attention to the dream of the energy, I was giddy and excited.

I dreamt and in the dream flowing gently through consciousness was energy unbounded.

I dreamt of form and shape.

I dreamt of beginning and end.

I dreamt of up and of down.

I dreamt of blackness and light.

I dreamt a million colors, a billion songs, and a trillion forms.

It was beautiful, wondrous, fractal, exploding.

It was corpuscles of color and light beyond anything ever seen before.

It was amazing!

It was wonder!

It was bliss.

It was joy.

It was fun, but unfortunately, the fun did not last.

The fun could not last.

It would not matter how creative and imaginative I might have been, or how flexible the energy, or how varied the experience.

It would not matter what I did.

With an eternity to explore and no beginning and no end, eventually "it" would happen again.

No matter how brilliant and creative the dream, no matter how fractal and varied the dance, I would eventually become bored.

It was inevitable because it is the nature of consciousness in eternity. When you have an eternity to ponder, boredom is inevitable. And so it happened that when I had explored all permutations and combinations, when I had imagined all the colors and shades of the rainbow, when all shapes had been created, and all transitions fully mapped, when I had done all the math and exhausted all the possibilities (twice and thrice), when there was nothing left to do and no new thoughts to think, boredom set in once again.

I Am the "I" in Creation

And I can tell you with little doubt this second boredom was a bigger problem, because when it finally occurred, when I had run out of things to think about, I did not have any idea how to proceed.

I could not, for example, expand on the Water of Creation.

I could not make the toy any better.

The Plasticine of Paradise was already wonderful. It was already infinitely pliable and it would already do anything and everything that I could imagine. The Water of Creation was already the perfect mirror of Divine will and I simply couldn't improve on that.

But I couldn't stand still either.

I had run out of good dreams to dream, boredom had set in, and the anguish of eternal ennui would be soon to follow.

I had to find something to do.

But what?

It was a bit of a stumper, but of course I was not worried.

The solution would eventually present itself.

It was inevitable.

Within the boundary-less nature of eternity, no problem is insurmountable and so I thought and I thought and I thought and finally *inspiration* struck and an idea emerged. If I couldn't go back to the blissful navel gazing of I, and if I couldn't improve on the energy in mind, the only thing to do was to add another "eye" to creation.

Yes, I thought excitedly, adding another "eye" was *the key*.

Adding another eye would add a new factor to the equation.

Adding another eye would add a new view on manifestation.

Adding another eye would add another *perspective* on creation.

It was genius.

It was fantastic.

It was brilliant!

It was the perfect solution and *the only* way forward.

With a new perspective on creation, with a new way of looking at the energy, it would all be different. Creation would start from exactly the same spot (i.e. as quiescent Water waiting for the ideas and intent of consciousness (i.e. the Word of God) to begin the process) but would end in a totally different location. The path that we would take would be different than the path that I had traveled.

From our unique perspectives we would work together and create entirely new universes never before conceived.

We would waltz through creation and manifest a universe of new possibilities.

Instead of a solitary jig we'd have a cooperative jiggle.

It would be fantastic.

It would be fun.

It would be wonderful.

But...

I am God

...before I got too excited...

Before "I" become "we" and "our" dance of creation could begin, I would have to iron out a couple of implementation details. I couldn't just instantiate a new eye without thinking,

70

right? Since adding a new eye changed the fundamental nature of The Fabric of Consciousness, since adding a new eye would mean that creation was no longer the solitary dream of "I", adding a new eye was a big deal and I wanted to get it right, so a little creative planning was in order.

I had to ask myself the obvious questions.

Where would I add the new eye?

What view of creation would it take?

From what perspective would it peer?

These were necessary questions and I needed good answers, otherwise I'd be back to boredom too quickly, and I didn't want that, so I needed to add the right perspective.

But what did the "right perspective" entail?

Well, obviously, I did not want to add an identical perspective. Creating an identical eye in exactly the same spot and looking from exactly the same point as the original "I" would not make sense at all.

It would add no variation: It would bring no deviation.

It would be like multiplying a mathematical equation by one.

The bottom line was, if I added a new eye in exactly the same place looking at exactly the same view from exactly the same vantage point, I would get exactly the same results as before.

The universe would unfold on an identical path.

Oh sure, perhaps with two eyes I would change things around a bit, but even so there could be only limited variation. With two eyes looking from the same perspective I'd see things the same way and because of that I'd make the same decisions in pretty much the same order as the first time.

I would do it all over again, and that would be B.O.R.I.N.G. So, obviously, I would have to add a different perspective.

But different in what way?

It was a stumper, I agree, but, a little eternity, a little air, a little fire, and I solved the problem in simple and elegant fashion. And all I had to do was acquire a little bit of self-knowledge. All I had to do was realize that **I AM GOD** and from my original perspective **I WAS Omniscient,** meaning that being the only being to exist, and having only *my* thoughts for amusement, I was conscious of everything that existed all at once.

I knew everything that I was thinking, and thus I knew everything that existed.

Since I was the only one to exist, if it was in my mind, I knew about it.

In this early stage of creation I knew everything that there was to know.

I was aware, eternal, blissful, powerful and, to top it all off, omniscient.

It made perfect philosophical sense.

It was one big circle, really. In fact, it was a lot like the snake Ouroboros that eats its own tail. Consciousness, imagination, inspiration, energy, and the manifestation from that energy are all part of the same pulsating consciousness that forever finds fuel and oxygen for the fire by consuming its own internal resources in an unending and oh-so-eternal cycle of self-awareness, inspiration, and bliss.

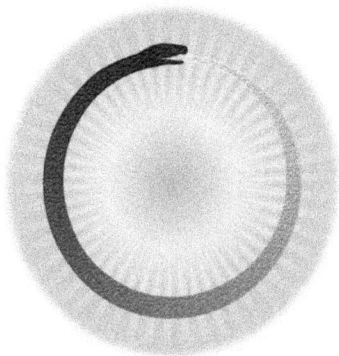

I am sure you will *see* at this point!

I AM, we are, a self-contained and self-perpetuating creation.

Now that wasn't so hard, was it?

And isn't that a grand and glorious realization!

The only question now is, if I could see everything, if I was omniscient and all potent, what change could be made that would bring interest and variation? What new variation could be created that would fuel inspiration, fire imagination, and solve the problem of boredom? What would, what could, the new perspective be like?

Part Three
Everything from the
Perspective of Consciousness

I Am the "Eye" in Creation

At this point I suppose the answer to the question of the new perspective should be obvious. If the view of "eye" as God was total and omniscient, then in order to ensure variation and deviation in creation, the view of other "eye" and "other God" would have to be "not total" and "not omniscient."

It would work like this.

If old "eye" saw the big picture, "new I" would see only a part.

If old "eye" was all-seeing, "new eye" would be limited.

If old "eye" was omniscient, "new eye" (otherwise known as you) would not be.

It was the only thing that would work.

A new eye with a new, but slightly limited, view was the only way forward.

It was the only thing that would guarantee a new dance, and so when the new eye, the "other eye" was instantiated, there would be a restriction of perspective and a narrowing of the vista. It was a perfect solution to the problem of eyes and a perfect way to add complexity to the equation.

Of course, there is a bit of a problem here. Instantiating a new eye with a limited perspective could lead to a jealous reaction and ongoing issues with self-esteem. After all, what new "eye" in The Fabric, would be happy being "less than" the original eye? The truth is, no new "eye" would ever find that acceptable.[26] To allow such a situation to stand would import hierarchy and superiority into the equation, and that would not be acceptable at all. No manner of excuse and justification could ever make that right. Therefore, something had to be done: something had to be offered in exchange. At first it was a bit of quandary. A reduction in perspective necessarily represented a reality of less than, and how could you make up for that? Of course, with an eternity to ponder no problem ever goes unsolved, and so after a while the solution became obvious. If new "eye" could not be equally omniscient, new "eye" could instead provide greater detail. One perspective would be wide but broad; the other perspective would narrow, but more detailed!

It would be like using a magnifying glass to build a model ship!

The view without the magnifying glass would be like the original omniscient view of I/GOD. You could hold the ship at arm's length and view the entire structure front to back, top to bottom. You could be aware of the depth and breadth, the entire ship, in one efficient, "omniscient" gaze. However, pick up a magnifying glass and look through it and you would no longer be able to view the entire ship. Your view would be,

---

[26] Unless of course you lied to the new "eye" so that it had an erroneous view of its position. But that would not work for long. Being part of the Fabric of Consciousness, new "eye" would either eventually see the truth for itself, or eventually connect with the knowledge of its inferiority and limitation. Either way, the truth would eventually come out.

in relation to the original omniscient perspective of eye, limited. Nevertheless the limited view would not be less than, it would just be more focused.

Old "eye" might see broad strokes and wide vistas, but new "eye" would perceive fine detail and subtler features.

Old "eye" would see the whole ship; new "eye" would see the details in the rigging.

Old "eye" might paint the hull; new "eye" might carve the detail into the molding.

The truth was new "eye," with magnifying glass in hand, would, as a result of its more focused perspective, be able to see things, do things, and accomplish things that old "eye," with its broader but less detailed view, could not.

New "eye" would see less, but more!

It was a wonderful thing!

With magnifying glass in hand, new "eye" would be able to add a level of realism to your creation simply not possible before.

Different, but equal, and never inferior! It was a perfect solution and it leveled the playing field immediately, for in truth while both perspectives were different, neither was superior. The broad big picture view of original "eye" would provide overview and perspective, but the narrow, more focused view of new "eye" would provide granularity and fascinating detail. New "eye" would not be omniscient, it is true, but in exchange for the limitation of view it would see more of its lesser area, and that was wonderful beyond imagination not only because of the variation in work but because of the information exchanged as a result. With a new perspective, with a new view, new information, new inspiration, and new possibilities could emerge.

Indeed, arguably, new "eye," because of its new perspective, would be **more important** than the old I in every way because it would be new "eye" that would permit the variation and deviation. It would be the new "eye" and only the new "eye" that could visualize a new creation, and add playful creative interest that the old "eye," the "god eye," the omniscient (but terribly old sod) "eye" simply could no longer provide. The bottom line was, having "been there and done that" old "eye" would unfold creation in the same old boring manner as I had done before. And that would be unspeakably B.O.R.I.N.G.

Now, those of you with some form of prior "training" may be scratching your heads at this point. Invariably, world religions teach that the original perspective (the perspective of God) is the important one. "They" teach that only God's views matter. "They" teach that the littler ones (the narrower views) are limited and limiting and should therefore be, among other things, compliant and subservient.

It is logical, they say, and necessary. For the "little ones" are *less than* the big one.

They are broken, they are stupid, they are "descended," they are servants, they are sheep, they are cattle, they are lambs, and they shall necessarily kneel, "they" say.

You can believe what "they" say if you want, but "I" am telling you now, those particular views have nothing to do with cosmic Truth and everything to do with the hierarchies of power and privilege of Earth. Saying that old "eye" wants you to kneel and that old "eye" wants you to serve is not Truth, but justification. It justifies and supports compliance to earthly authority and nothing more. You can believe it if you want, but it only serves to bind you in the end. And in any case it makes no logical or cosmological sense. Adding a new "eye" that is subservient and compliant, adding a new "eye" that is less than the original "eye," besides the fact that it would be inconceivable to a consciousness that is all love, light, and bliss, would defeat the purpose altogether. After all, the purpose of instantiating a new "eye" is to create a new perspective that would *add* creative variation. To add a new "eye" that linked up with, and was subservient to, old "eye" would not accomplish the goal. It would circumvent creative variation, undermine deviation, and prevent a new creative unfolding from occurring. There would be no point to it. It would be, in short, boring. And nobody, least of all old "eye" (who's already been there and done that) wants that. [27]

---

[27] So why do "they" teach that new "eye" (that's you) are less than old "I?" Why do they teach that the new eyes are fallen from grace or ejected from the Garden? Why do they teach that new eyes are descended from apes? Why participate in such a magnificently executed but horrible and tragic lie? Dear one, it is merely to keep

Eye + I + Will

And so, there you have it. You now know that the solution to ennui after the instantiation of the Waters of Creation was to

---

you in bondage. They teach you these lies because they are part of an ancient System (the System, as I like to say) that extracts your energy, concentrates it in the hands of a few, all the while keeping you away from your power and glory. It is a powerful system, and a pernicious system, and it erases the obvious and true from your minds. Think about it. We are not born onto this earth wanting to work! We are born onto this earth wanting to play! As you must know, play is the prime directive of every child, on every planet, in every system, in every universe. It is the Purpose of creation, it is the **Point** of manifestation, and it is not so easy to make a soul forget the Point. It is only after years of physical and mental violence, and constant "pushing away of the spirit," that our bodies learn that work is what makes us valuable. It takes a long time and an incredible and coordinated effort to accomplish this twist. You have to lie to the children and say they are good for nothing, broken, filled with sin, and inferior. You have to scare them with your power and threaten them with damnation. You have to do horrible things (and more) and tell all these god-awful lies until they finally forget who they are, hand you their power, and kneel in compliance and obedience. There was a reason for it all of course (see The Book of Life: Ascension and the Divine World Order), so it is not appropriate to stand in judgment, or invoke punishment, but it is time to put aside greed, graft, corruption, and bodily ego and embrace the glorious truth of our unity and oneness in the wondrous Fabric of Consciousness.

create another "eye," another perspective, to perceive creation with. It was simple and elegant. Before moving on, however, there is one other traditional "teaching" that requires clarification. In order to accomplish this, we'll have to bring forward the understanding that by adding a new eye to creation, by adding a new "you" to the Fabric of Consciousness, I was not simply adding a solitary "eye" in isolation from other aspects of consciousness. That is, I was not simply adding a new perspective or a new view. It wasn't like adding a new eye to the back of your head. I was also adding a new "I" (a **new identity**), and **a new will** (the power to make decisions and get things done) I was, in short, adding a new "head" or a new "ego" [28] to the Fabric of Consciousness and this new head would be independent (though not separate) from the original, It would be its own unique ego and it would have, most importantly, full access to the full gamut of capabilities in consciousness.

I suppose the question at this point is, why would I need to add a new "I," and a new will, to the "eye" in creation? Could I not continue to go it alone and simply use the new information provided by the new perspectives (the new "eye") to make a new creation?

Would not the new and independent stream of data be enough?

---

[28] When you have a unique perspective, plus a unique identity, plus a fully functional will, you have what we may call a complete **ego**. I would thus like to define ego as follows:

Ego = Eye + I + Will.

The answer to that question is no.

The basic problem here was one of independence. If all I add are new "eyes" to the equation, I leave out a significant component of a fully operating perspective–namely a sense of identity ("I") and will. If all I add is a new eye, all I am really doing is giving myself a little magnifying glass so that I may look upon my creation from a different perspective. While this may add some interest and allow some variety the second time around, it is a less than optimal solution. Adding a new eye with a narrower focus will allow me to see the details it is true, but in the end, and from my omniscient perspective, I will still be making all the decisions.

At first glance this might not seem like a problem, but if you think about it for a moment you will see that it is. If I am making all the decisions then, given the fact that I've already unfolded creation from a single perspective and I've already "been there and done that," my next time around will be largely identical to the first time. Given my previous experience, I will make the best choices possible and unfold creation in the most interesting way the second time around. I'll follow the paths of most excitement, avoid the byways that lead to nowhere interesting, and I'll go pretty much exactly the same way as I did before. Even if I did not, I'd still have already done everything. It would be much like driving to work by yourself every day. Having been there and done that a thousand times, you would eventually settle into a rut of efficiency. It would not take long for you to find the ideal time to leave, the best route to work, and the most efficient way back home; and no matter how many new passengers you added to the car, as long as you, the driver, are making all the decisions, there will be limited stimulus to change the route. It will be the same old, same old pretty much every day.

This is exactly how it would be for me if I didn't do anything except add new eyes. The new "drive" through creation would be slightly more interesting (I'd be able to see more this time around, for example), but the route would not change much. In the end, if all the passengers did was sit there and look pretty, it would get pretty boring, pretty quickly. It is for this reason that it was necessary to add an independent "I" to the new "eye". Adding new egos and giving each new ego total independence was the only thing that would ensure that the new unfolding of creation would be unique. Adding an independent *will* would be the difference between a solitary drive to work and a carpool where everyone in the car is making decisions based on all the new things they want to see. With more drivers making decisions, you'll be taking detours, leaving at different times, and generally unfolding your trip in a totally novel manner. It would be new every day if everybody is involved and attentive and equal.

And so there you have it, and so that is what "I" would have to do. In order to bring creative interest to the equation I would add a new ego, that is: a new "eye," plus a new "I," plus an independent will. We'll get to the outcome of this in a moment, but now let us pause for a moment and define "eye" plus "I." For the sake of simplicity let us, from this point forward, refer to the unique combination of ("I+eye+will") by the common name of *monad*.[29] A monad is basically a unique perspective ("eye"), a complete sense of identify ("I"), and the will to get things done. From this point forward we will use the term monad (or ego) to describe an "eye+I+will".[30] We can define the word Monad and Ego thus.

Definition: Monad

Monad = Eye + I + Will

Ego = Eye + I + Will

---

[29] See http://www.thespiritwiki.com/index.php/Monad

[30] It is important you wrap your head around these three elements because they form the basis of that little thing we call "me." In order for "me" to exist, in order for the concept of "me" to have any meaning at all, "me" must have a unique perspective (or view), a unique sense of identity (or I) and a unique will. If you were a human being we could say that to be fully human you needed to have Eye + I + Will. This would mean that any social, political, or economic conditions that denied any of these three things would make you "less than" human and therefore a disjunctive sin against The Fabric. But to say you are only human is to deny your true identity as Light in the Fabric. Therefore we might more accurately say that to be fully instantiated as a spiritual monad you must have Eye + I + Will. Only when these three things are present are you fully actuated as spiritual ego.

Eye
Eye + Eye

And that is really all there is to it! At this point it should all seem pretty straightforward. With an eternity on your hands, boredom is inevitable, and finding ways to overcome that boredom is the primary problem and the point of creative endeavor. In this context, adding a monad to creation seemed like the perfect solution. At this point there was only one consideration left over and that was, how many new monads would "I" like to add.

Should only one monad be added, or ten?

Should a thousand new monads be added, or a trillion?

It took only a moment's consideration to realize that adding only a single new monad would not be that useful. If I only added one new eye to the Fabric of Consciousness, only a smaller part of creation, only one side of the Unfolding, would be viewable in detail. The other side, the side that the new eye was not looking at, would remain unobserved. Remember, the new eye is not omniscient. It does not see all things at once. It only sees "a part" of creation. The "other part" that it does not see would remain in darkness. Not total darkness, of course. Original "I" would still see it as from above, and so there'd still be a view of the entire creative sphere, but with only one new eye operating in detail view, many of the potential features in creation would be missed. This will become clear if we consider the example of our ship once again. Taking the ship in hand you will recall that the view of original "I" was as "from afar." The original omniscient perspective was holding the ship at arm's length and seeing all sides. The view of any new monad holding a magnifying glass would be different. With magnifying glass in hand, the new monad would see the details of the ship, but with only one magnifying glass available, the new monad would really only be able to examine one side of the ship at a time. There would be thus gaps in the detailed apprehension of the ship. But that wasn't a problem. A little bit of thought and original "I" realized that more than one new monad could be easily accommodated and so that is what "I" did. In the "new beginning," and at the dawn of the new Unfolding, original monad added two new monads to creation. One new monad would look at one side of creation, and the other new monad would look at the other side, and variation, deviation, and creative interest would result. It was the perfect solution and so, with determination and resolution, original "I" turned attention from the energy.

And as The Waters stilled...

And as the energy settled...

I said (with as much bravado and bluster as I could muster for this magnificent and momentous moment in creation),

"LET THERE BE MORE LIGHT".

And with that, consciousness intensified, self-awareness ignited, and two new monads instantiated into existence.[31]

---

[31] I will call the *process* of invoking new monads in the Fabric the **intensification of consciousness**. Intensification occurs as a

And together we said:

WE ARE THE EYES ON CREATION

WE ARE THE I'S OF IDENTITY

WE ARE THE WILL AND THE MOTIVATION

WE ARE THE UNIQUE PERSPECTIVE OF MONADS

WE ARE THE ETERNAL UNFOLDING OF
CONSCIOUSNESS.

And with that we turned, and we focused, and our dance began.

And we smiled, for we saw that it was going to be good.

The Playing is The Thing

Of course, the first thing that I did when "I" became "we" was to get down to the business of play.

It is what we always did.

---

result of the "gathering of awareness" into a single point of intensified consciousness that is *self-aware* (i.e. aware of "I" or "me"). You can wrap your head around this process by imagining a room full of mist. The mist is consciousness. Now imagine little whirlpools in the mist. These whirlpools gather the mist of awareness (the Fabric of Consciousness) into increasingly dense points. At a certain point in the process of formation the point of awareness "ignites" and self-awareness is born. We can call the process of congelation to the point of self-awareness as the intensification of consciousness. I will call the actual birth of a self-aware monad the **instantiation of monadic consciousness**.

Play is The Point, after all, and so we played.

And let me tell you, it was wonderful.

It was fractal, scintillating, exploding.

With three monads working from three different perspectives (all dancing a dance of equality) we manifested entirely new worlds for our creative edification. And as we manifested, we danced, and we laughed, and we pushed, and we shoved, and we giggled, and we screamed, and we jumped, and we fell, and we explored the (almost) infinite permutations of our (almost) infinite creation.

And it was terrific fun, while it lasted.

But of course eventually, inevitably, "it" happened. After all, when you have an eternity of eternities to explore, even the (almost) unlimited possibilities of "we" are eventually exhausted. And as you already know, when the play gets boring and the dance a mere routine, we do what any self-respecting creator consciousness would do: We start looking around for something to bring back the fun again, and I'll tell you, at this point it only took a *single moment* to decide the way forward.

In order to alleviate the new boredom, in order to solve The Problem (i.e. in order to overcome the ennui), in order to bring the fun back into creation, we would simply create more monads. It was entirely within the realm of capability and besides, our previous experience moving from "I" to "we" convinced us that adding more monads was a great way to move forward. Adding new monads added detail, potential, variation, and deviation! In short, adding more monads added factors to the equation that increased the complexity and enhanced our experience.

It worked to overcome ennui last time, it would work again!

Adding more monads was the obvious way forward and so, after having grown bored of the solipsism of I, and having exhausted the potential of three, with no hesitation we raised our collective voices and declared:

"LET THERE BE MORE LIGHT!"

And with that, twelve new monads came into existence.

And together we said:

WE ARE THE EYES ON CREATION

WE ARE THE I'S OF IDENTITY

WE ARE THE WILL AND THE MOTIVATION

WE ARE THE UNIQUE PERSPECTIVE OF MONADS

WE ARE THE ETERNAL
UNFOLDING OF CONSCIOUSNESS.

And with that we turned, and we focused, and our dance began.

And we smiled, for we saw that it was going to be good.

We Are the Twelve of Heaven

Now I know what you are asking at this point (or at least I think I know).

Why twelve new monads?

Why not two or three or even a hundred more?

Why that exact number?

Well, for no other reason than twelve seemed like the right balance, and a good idea at the time. Adding two or three (or even five) new perspectives seemed a bit wishy-washy. It would add some complexity and variation, but we did not think it would be enough of a shift. It would be too much like our last addition and would not *stretch the imagination* enough to be interesting. At the same time, and on the other hand, we did not want to add too many new monads. If we added too many too soon, we would risk the possibility of being overwhelmed by the dramatic expansion in perspective and information flow, and get "lost" in the cacophony of ego. More to the point, if we added too many too soon we might miss out on some of the more interesting *interim stages* and qualitative shifts that would follow from just the right increase in "eye" and "I." We wanted to experience everything that could be experienced at each new "level" of the Unfolding.

Or at least, that's how we thought about it at that time.

Not too many, not too few, but just right.

So, in this context, and with this reasoning, twelve seemed like just the right number. It was not too many and not too few. It would add sufficient complexity, thereby challenging and stretching the fabric of imagination, but it would not be too much of a jump so that we would miss out on important creative permutations, or get lost in the cacophony of ego.

We are the Arc-Angles of Specialization

Of course, at this point it goes without saying that the new monads were going to be different than the previous monads. They had to be different, otherwise creation would stagnate; but, different in what way? Well, this time the answer to that question was easy. Unlike the first time "I" added new monads, unlike the first time I *unfolded* consciousness, no extended consideration was required. The answer was already there. When we were ready the three simply looked at what "I" had done previously and simply duplicated that. Last time, as you will recall, "I" added two new monads with a narrower, but more detailed view of creation in order to increase complexity and introduce variety. This time "we" would do exactly the same. This time we would add twelve new eyes, twelve narrower, but more detailed, views of creation, and in this addition we would create new possibility and new potential.

And of course we knew it would be great.

Adding new monads with narrower, but more detailed, views would add deviation and variation. With twelve we would not be confined to a single omniscient overview, or two opposite detail views. We would be adding twelve narrower views and these, like the slices of a pie, would focus on twelve different angles. If "the Two" had seen opposite sides of creation, "the Twelve" new "arc-angles" of creation would see creation in sections and from different angles of view. Of course, it goes without saying that the arc-angles would be an important addition. Just like the addition of opposite views in the previous creative step added deviation and variation, the new arc-angles would do the same. They would be critical because the fresh information that they would provide, and the new perspectives that they would bring, would ensure that creation would unfold along a unique and fun-filled path. It should also go without saying at this point that the twelve new arc-angles of creation would not be created *less than* or *subservient* in any way. Adding new, but subservient, monads would undermine the potential for new deviation and variation, create jealousy in the playground, and would ultimately defeat the purpose. Therefore the Twelve would have to be created as equals. Indeed, it would always have to be like this. At no matter what point in the Unfolding we might be, no matter how many monads we might eventually add, it would always be technically necessary to create equality of "I," "eye," and will. Thus when we added the twelve new monads we added them with equality, respect, and awareness that without their contribution we'd all be furiously and frantically bored.

I suppose now is a good time to pause for a visual overview of this expanding Fabric of Consciousness. Remember we started off with one "I", added two more (I+I), and then moved on to twelve. All together that gives us, at this point in the Unfolding, fifteen perspectives organized into three "levels" of creation. If we were to illustrate this unfolding with a series of capital "I's" (one for each monad) and organize the levels into a pyramid, the pyramid would look something like the figure below, with the top level of I being the perspective of omniscience, the second level of two being the perspective of opposites, and the third level of twelve being the arc-angles of a now continuously unfolding Fabric of Consciousness.

The Pyramid of Creation

I

II

IIIIIIIIIIII

At this point in the Unfolding we have fifteen monads, three "levels", and one wondrous creation stretched out before us in unlimited, unrealized potential. Put another way, we have a bunch of monads intending in creation and bringing massive variation and vast unexplored new potential into the equation. Wonderful! And I am sure that by this point we do not have to be told what we were going to do with this potential. We were going to play, and so that is what we did. Immediately upon instantiation of the twelve new arc-angles we got down to the serious business of play and exploration. We dreamt, and the dream flowing gently through consciousness was of energy unbounded.

We dreamt of dancing and prancing, of form and of shape.

We dreamt of beginning and end and of up and down.

We dreamt in darkness and in exploding light.

It was beautiful, wondrous, fractal, exploding.

It was amazing!

It was wonder!

It was bliss.

It was joy.

And it was fun...

...while it lasted.

But of course, it could not last forever. With an eternity to explore and no beginning and no end, eventually we would become bored. It was simply in the nature of consciousness.

But, not to worry!

When we get bored we always knew just what to do. We would draw away from the energy, we would turn to each other, and we would say...

"LET THERE BE MORE LIGHTS!"

...and there would be more.

The only question at this point was, how many more?

Should it be twenty-four?

Should it be forty-eight?

Of course, we didn't want to be overwhelmed with new information flow, but at the same time we did want to ensure enough new perspectives to guarantee deviation and variation. Not too many, not too few. The problem at this point was however that we were getting the hang of it. From one to three to fifteen the process, the challenges, and the outcome were well understood, almost boring. At this point adding only twenty-four, or forty-eight, or even one hundred and forty four didn't seem like it would do the trick.

It was like the technical mastery of a virtuoso piano player, fascinating to watch, but automatic to the player.

It wasn't a "stretch" for our imagination anymore, and that was bad because imagination is critical.

Imagination is what fuels the fire.

Imagination is what guarantees wondrous and glorious new creations.

Without imagination, everything stays the same. And that is boring. Therefore, to ensure continued fuel for the fire a bigger jump seemed warranted. A bigger jump would not only add perspective, deviation and variation, but the massive increase in information flow would require more than just automated response. It would bring additional challenge and it would fuel the fires of imagination. Thus, and after some careful consideration, we decided that in the new round of the Unfolding there would be many more new monads, enough to create an exponential increase in information flow, and enough to bring technical challenge to the process of creation.

How many more would we add?

After a bit of consideration, we the Fifteen decided that we would add one thousand seven-hundred and twenty-eight (1,728) new monads, with narrower but more detailed perspectives.

We Are the Angelic Multitude

Now I know what you are thinking at this point.

Why this exact number?

Why 1,728 and not 1,741?

Why 1,728 and not 100?

Well, it really was an issue of practicality and planning. Since we had already added three and twelve, we needed to move beyond this "basic" level of complexity. We wanted to raise the creative stakes a bit. We wanted to kick it up a notch and adding twelve, or even twelve times twelve, did not seem like it would be enough of a stretch for the imagination. The bottom line was, we had worked with that factorial and would, if we were going to keep the game interesting, need a quantum leap beyond. Thus the question was, how many new monads would we have to add to provide a quantum leap forward? Thankfully, it did not take us much thought to figure it out. In fact, the answer hit us almost right away and we settled on twelve times twelve times twelve (12x12x12) new monads to add to the Fabric of Consciousness.

Twelve times twelve times twelve (or twelve cubed) would add the complexity we wanted to add.

Twelve cubed would ensure a quantum leap forward in complexity.

Twelve cubed would introduce a new challenge.

Twelve cubed would fan the fires of creation.

Twelve cubed was elegant and symmetrical.

To understand this, let us take another look at our pyramid of creation. Recall that just before we added 1,728 new monads, we were working with three levels in the pyramid. The first level was the original I, the second level our opposite perspectives, and the third our detailed arc-angles of creation. At the third level of creation the pyramid of consciousness looked like this.

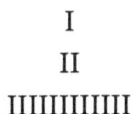

I

II

IIIIIIIIIII

To further our example, let us **drop the first two levels** out of the illustration for a moment, take only the bottom level of the pyramid, and expand that across the page like so.

I   I   I   I   I   I   I   I   I   I   I   I

Now remember, we are considering why we chose the number 12x12x12 and not simply 12x12, or some other number. If we only took twelve times twelve, we would only have one hundred and forty-four (144) new monads. If we divided the one hundred and forty-four equally among the twelve Little Ones we would only be able to add twelve monads under each of the twelve Little Ones.

If we did that, the third and fourth level of our pyramid of consciousness would look like this.

I   I   I   I   I   I   I   I   I   I
IIIIIIIII IIIIIIIII IIIIIIIII IIIIIIIII IIIIIIIII IIIIIIIII IIIIIIIII IIIIIIIII IIIIIIIII IIIIIIIII

As you can clearly see, this amounts to pretty much exactly the same expansion that occurred when we added twelve under two, as we did when we unfolded the third level of creation.

I

II

IIIIIIIIIII

By adding 12 x 12 monads at the fourth level of the unfolding, we would only be adding twelve to one, as you can clearly see. This would be pretty much the same thing, and since we had already worked with that level of complexity we needed to do something more. Thus, instead of adding 12 x 12 new monads (thereby only giving us twelve underneath each third level monad), we would cube the number of little ones at the bottom and add twelve times twelve for each of the twelve third level monads. Thus, instead of this:

I   I   I   I   I   I   I   I   I   I

IIIIIIIIII IIIIIIIIII IIIIIIIIII IIIIIIIIII IIIIIIIIII IIIIIIIIII IIIIIIIIII IIIIIIIIII IIIIIIIIII IIIIIIIIII

We would have this:

I   I   I   I   I   I   I   I   I   I

12x12 12x12 12x12 12x12 12x12 12x12 12x12 12x12 12x12 12x12

Or, if you prefer, this:

I   I   I   I   I   I   I   I   I   I

144   144   144   144   144   144   144   144   144   144

And this would most certainly be a quantum leap forward in complexity.

Now, when you connect the dots, plug the numbers in, and perform the necessary calculations, at the fourth level of the Unfolding you have a total of one thousand seven-hundred and twenty-eight new monads in creation (12x12x12=1,728). Add them all together and you get a grand total of 1,743 monads.

Laid out in formula, it looks like this.

$$1+2+12+(\mathbf{12x12x12})=1,743$$

or

$$1+2+12+(\mathbf{1728})=1743$$

Laid out in "level" format it looks like this.

$$1$$
$$2$$
$$12$$
$$1,728$$

I'm sure you will agree that with this many new monads we succeed in our primary goal of ensuring a quantum leap forward.[32] With this many monads, we would definitely have

---

[32] In case some of you are questioning the relevance of talking

added variety, granularity, detail, and complexity.

The permutations would be near infinite.

The deviation would be exciting.

The variation would be stunning.

It meant an exponential explosion of creative possibility, and a quantum leap forward in creative potential. It was great,

---

about "number" in this fashion here, I just want to point out that Isidor Kalisch (2006 (1877)) says, according to the Sepher Yetirah (SY) that G-D calls creation into existence by quantity and quality. Kalisch suggests that quantity is represented by the thirty-two letters of the Hebrew alphabet which form the thirty-two ways or paths of divine wisdom. Kalisch also suggests quality is represented by the twelve sephiroth. I would say that in the glorious creative emanation that is the Unfolding of Consciousness, *quantity* refers merely to the expanding number of instantiated monads in the Fabric while *quality* refers to the emergence of the "dimensions" of creation. We already know that the number of monads is important. Monads bring required depth, perspective, and detail to the creative equation. The number of monads determines, in a very real way, the type of creation we are able to create. With only one instantiated monad, creation is necessarily simple (and ultimately boring). However, adding more monads adds creative variation and potential. It is ultimately the quantitative addition of monads that makes the Universe that you see around you possible, hence the emphasis on number in SY and this BOL. We'll see this clearly as we progress through this four volume Book of Light.

In the next section we will introduce you to the Book of Light equivalent of quality/sephiroth. In volume three of this series we will look in some detail at the vibratory creation of the physical universe (what in Sepher Yetzirah is characterized as G-D speaking) and look how the "word of God" is the foundation for all of creation.

and as we thought about it we realized with this many monads we could now create a universe of unparalleled beauty, detail, and complexity! We would be like the finest wood craftsman or the most skilled mason. With this many eyes we could add exquisite detail. No longer would we paint creation in the broad brushstrokes of a small number of limited perspectives. Now we would paint with the detailed pixilation of the most powerful earth-based supercomputer.

We would have to.

How else would we exploit the possibilities provided by the addition of 1,728 new monads? And so, this is what we did. We instantiated 1,728 new monads and, with creation in mind, we got down to the business of play and exploration. And of course, we were all very hopeful and excited; but unfortunately, we didn't get too far into our creative play before we noticed that something was different about the way creation was working.

It was quite odd.

Something had changed!

Something was wrong!!

As we looked closer we could see the problem. The Water of Creation was no longer responding as we expected. Specifically, energy was no longer responding according to the foundational laws of creation which were, as you will recall,

1. Energy shall have no limitation

2. Energy shall respond to intent (as above in

consciousness, so below in matter)

3. Energy's response shall be instant and literal.

Put another way, the Waters of Creation were no longer responding in a literal, reflective, or responsive manner!!

Something had gone horribly wrong.

It was a bit of a shocker, especially considering that the Water of Creation does what it does because of its nature as an aspect of "I". Since the nature of "I" hadn't changed at all (adding new monads was merely a *quantitative* change), the Water should not have changed. But it did, and so clearly deeper investigation was in order.

Part Four
Dimensions/Sephiroth of Creation

We Randomize

I have to admit, this change in creation, this alteration in the way energy was responding to intent, was an interesting development and altogether unexpected. To be perfectly honest, we the 1,743 monads (henceforth to be known as Immortal Spirit) had thought that the Unfolding would just continue in a straightforward and linear fashion with no alteration and no changes for ever and ever amen. We had made the energy, after all, and felt that because of its nature (as reflected in the Three Laws), there would be no changes unless we intended a change. But now here we were experiencing a totally unintended and unexpected change in the functioning of the energy.

So, we investigated. We turned our attention to the energy, experimented with some simple manifestations, and quickly determined that "the change" was not so much a change in nature, but an addition of a characteristic, a change of *quality* in the energy. As we fiddled with manifestation and altered our parameters, we noticed that an additional factor had been added to the creative equation. A new condition had emerged that altered the way intent was manifesting in energy. You might say that a new *dimension* had been created that added additional complication and variation over and above what the simple quantitative increase of monads "should" have added. In fact, let's say just that. Let us say that at the fourth level of the Unfolding, when twelve times twelve times twelve new monads had been added to the equation, a qualitative shift in the energy occurred and a new dimension[33] of creation emerged out the increasingly complex Fabric of Consciousness.

And just what was this new dimension?

Before we get around to naming this new dimension (or new Sephiroth), we need to take a step back and remind ourselves of what we might like to call the default technical *foundation* of our creative work. That is, you have to recall how creation worked in the beginning (i.e., before the funny new dimension) to fully understand the new change and its implications. Fortunately, we have already gone over this, so it won't be hard. Recall the original relationship between god with a little "g" (also known as "I", or) and the energy of creation as stated in the Three Laws of Creation.

1. Energy shall have no limitation

2. Energy shall respond to intent (as above in consciousness, so below in matter)

3. Energy's response shall be instant and literal.

Remember, it is a direct connection. While these three laws are in operation energy is flexible, reflective, and responsive. These qualities emerge out of the nature of energy. Because energy is simply a dream inside the mind of "I" there is no barrier or distinction, no disconnect, between thought and

_____

[33] In Sepher Yetzirah shifts in the quality of the energy are represented by Sephiroth. Here they will be represented as *dimensions* of creation.

manifestation.

The relationship between energy and thought is direct and unmitigated.

Remember, the Water is merely a thought/dream inside the mind of God. Thus there is a fundamental unity between God and energy (creation) that governs the way energy responds.

God = energy = Thought = energy = God.

If the mind of God changes, the energy changes instantly and with no equivocation. The Water of Creation is always a direct (and perfect!) *reflection* of the mind of God. Because the Water of Creation is nothing more than a dream inside the mind of God it *must always be this way*. It can never, ever, ever change.

Now, it is this instant connection, this direct route from consciousness to manifestation, that I *call the default technical foundation of creation* (or simply the Foundation for short). In the beginning, when energy and mind are one, creation manifests instantly and literally. I'm not telling you anything you don't already know. I'm simply highlighting the basic truth of creation (i.e., God and Creation are one) and calling attention to the important creative implications of this relationship, which is instant and literal manifestation.

Creation is consciousness/Consciousness is creation.

It is important to note here that this basic principle of creation, this instant and literal linkage between consciousness and energy, operates throughout the levels of creation. Energy, because it is never more or less than a thought/dream/idea in the mind of God, *always* responds instantly and literally to intent. It is important to remember this, and important to understand that this is always the case.

It never changes.

And how could it anyway?

Energy is merely a dream inside the mind of "I."

Change the dream and you change manifestation and there's absolutely nothing, within the hallways of creation that can stop it.

The Mind of God is powerful, pre-emptive, and prevailing.

Now, pay attention to this next part because it is important.

Just because I say that the way that energy responds to intent (i.e., instantly and literally) never changes doesn't mean it never changes! You see, there is a practical wrinkle in this default technical foundation of creation, a creative hiccup that undermines (or at least seems to undermine) the direct relationship between I and creation. What is most interesting is that this hiccup did not exist in the beginning. This wrinkle (and all its derivatives) only appears when there is more than one monad looking at creation and it only becomes significant when there are many monads looking at creation. To put it as mysteriously as possible, things get a little complicated, and instant manifestation begins an illusory disintegration, when "I" becomes "we."

At first the changes are subtle and hardly perceptible. However, as the Unfolding progresses, the change accumulates to the point where it (i.e. the change) *pops* into our awareness. In the case of the change we are talking about here, the "pop" occurs at the fourth level...

$$1$$

$$2$$

$$12$$

$$1,728$$

...which, as you already know, is where we realized that creation was no longer following *the Laws of Creation*. It was at the fourth level that we all realized that manifesting was no longer a simple process of *intend and ye shall receive*. A complication had been entered that created the illusion that the Laws of Creation were being changed.

I've put it off long enough so now I'll just come right out and say it.

At the fourth level of the Unfolding when we had 1,728 monads working on creation, a qualitative shift occurred and a new dimension (or new Sephiroth) was added to creation that we shall call *chance*.

That is, at the fourth level of the Unfolding, the dimension of chance came into existence.

To put it another way, at the fourth level of the Unfolding, at the point where we added 1,728 monads, "random events" in the Fabric started to occur.

At the fourth level we intended just like we had always done, but the energy was no longer responding in a literal fashion. Weird things that we didn't expect, and that nobody had technically intended, began to happen.

As I said, it was a bit of a surprise.

Instead of energy always responding in a literal fashion, a certain uncertainty had been introduced into the process.

At this point I know it sounds weird and inexplicable, but don't fret. It is not as complicated or as esoteric as you might think, and there is a reasonable explanation for it. In fact, it will be much easier to understand if we suppress the incorrigible left brain and draw on the expansive right brain for assistance. Since the left brain responds primarily to words and thought, we can get around your incorrigible left brain by visualizing an image.

Visuals go straight to the right brain for processing.

So, let's do that.

Let us go straight to the right, brain that is.

Imagine for a moment that you are alone in a room with a bucket of paint, brushes, and a fresh blank canvas stretched out in front of you.

No problem here.

Being alone is great.

While you are alone, you are free to paint what you want, when you want. You have an idea, and you paint that idea instantly and without delay. You simply pick up your brush, dab it in the paint, and splash it on *your* canvas as *you* will. Nobody is there to criticize or judge, make suggestions, or fiddle with the thing. Nobody is there to get in the way.

There is, you might say, a **purity of will** when it comes to painting a solo canvas, at least in the beginning.

Now imagine that a dozen or more painters suddenly come into the room wanting to paint on the same white canvas. At first, everyone is excited by the possibility of painting and they do their own thing in isolation (it is a big canvas after all). They throw paint, wave brushes, smudge with their fingers and generally explore the multitude of creative possibilities on the canvas in front of them. They are independent, "at a distance," and not so much interested in the work of others. In this way, the painting (creation) emerges as a result of the chaotic manifestation of individual wills in isolation on the canvas. In this situation, and despite the presence of others painting on the canvas, purity of will[34] is precariously maintained.

This isolation does not go on for very long, however, because pretty soon some of the painters begin to get bored of painting in isolation and they start to look around at what others are doing. They nudge in towards their colleagues to look and as they do that, they begin to paint perilously close to the imaginings of other painters. As they continue to move in closer and as they get *right up close and personal* with the others, the painters notice an oddity. "Things" are now happening to their painting that they had not anticipated. The canvas is all connected, you see, and there are no natural boundaries[35] between the work of one and the work of

---

[34] When "will is pure" intent is reflected in energy in a direct and unmitigated fashion.

[35] Boundaries *can* be created but the borders are always more or less permeable depending on various conditions. Although you

another. As the painters get closer, and as each paints their vision, the colors they splash bleed over onto the work of the others. When this occurs, things begin to happen that were not intended, and creation unfolds in unexpected ways on the canvas. When painters get close to each other, and when their paint starts splashing the canvas of others, purity of will is forever lost. What is even "worse," the closer the painters get to each other, the less certain each painter is of manifesting exactly what they imagine onto the canvas. As we quickly learn, the closer we are to someone else, the more likely they are to do something that "messes" things up.

Let us extend our example.

Say you are painting in blue. You wave your brush in broad strokes creating blue form and blue shape. It is all fine and good until Charlie, who had been painting in blue right beside you up until a moment ago, gets bored and decides that he'd rather paint in red. He picks up a bucket full of red paint and flamboyantly splashes that paint over his own area on the blue canvas. The splash is so dramatic, and the paint ejected with such force, that his red spatters and runs into your blue.

Something happens that neither of you had intended (a "chance" event), nor anticipated.

You immediately stop.

You turn and furrow your eyebrows in annoyance and look at

---

could, for example, strengthen your borders to protect you like an iron prison, you waste a lot of energy doing that.

him. You don't fret it too long and your ire doesn't last more than a moment because as you take a closer look at your canvas you notice that your blue painting now contains beautiful streaks and splashes of purple. It is a surprise to both of you and you both stop and stare at the canvas, not knowing what to think. However, after the surprise wears off you both laugh and find that neither of you are annoyed in the least by this "chance" occurrence. First of all, Charlie is only trying to have fun. He wasn't deliberately trying to mess up your work. He was just doing what is his God-given right to do. Secondly, it turns out that the chance event is not a bad thing anyway. As you look at the combined blue and red you realize you are fascinated and titillated by the emergent color. A new thing has happened, a new "wrinkle" has occurred, a new "factor", random chance, has emerged.

You realize the importance of this almost immediately.

The rules have been altered.

The relationship has been complicated.

The nature of your creative work (the nature of creation) has changed.

From this point on creation can no longer be the simple and literal manifestation of individual will. Random (or chance) events will now feed into creation in a way that nobody is going to be able to predict with absolute certainty.

And what fun it would be!

This new dimension of chance would add an element of the unknown to the creative process that would virtually guarantee deviation, variation, and ongoing creative interest.

This new dimension of chance, this emergent wrinkle in the Fabric of Consciousness, was an awesome development, and we were all quite excited about what this might mean for our creative play, and quite anxious to begin our exploration process.

What wonderful new worlds awaited us as the new-found dimension of chance began to operate in creation we could only guess at, but we knew it was going to be good.

At this point it is probably worthwhile to pause a moment or two to examine the implications of the emergence of chance in the Fabric. In particular we should look at the impact of chance on the "laws" of creation. With the expansion in the Fabric of Consciousness and the introduction of chance into the equation, the Laws of Creation are now undermined. In particular, the third law (which states that energy follows intent instantly and literally) begins an accelerating "collapse." With more and more monads painting on the canvas, random creation occurs. As random creation expands, as events occur on your canvas that were neither expected nor intended, it is simply no longer possible to say that energy is responding to intent instantly and literally. Now things are happening that are not intended, and the creative efforts that you engage in are no longer working out in a literal fashion. Now color is splashing and bleeding all over the space. The third law no longer holds.

At this point it is important to understand something. You can see that with the addition of more monads, chance is introduced as a dimension. You can also see the cause of this in the intentional and willful events of other monads. What is important to understand here is that while practically strict operation of the third law no longer holds, technically the energy is still responding in a literal fashion. In practical terms, the creative intent of proximal monads (i.e., monads interested in the sorts of things that you are doing) interferes, interjects, and otherwise intercepts and modifies the creative intent of another monad. Technically all changes that occur, no matter how random they are, started with the willful intent of one or more monads. If you and I are standing close to each other on the Canvas of Creation, and I splash paint, and that paint bleeds onto your area and changes your creation, a chance event has practically occurred, but technically that event can be traced directly to my actions.

Theoretically the rules stand, but practically they have fallen.

This may seem like a philosophical conundrum, but it is not. It may seem irrelevant now, but it becomes very important later on. Until then, the key to remember here is that even though chance has emerged as a new dimension of creation, nothing occurs in creation without the willful and directed intent of one or another monad. Put another way, from your perspective an event might seem like pure and random chance, but from the "highest" perspective there's always someone or another monad standing beside you, or behind you, with a paint brush splatting on your canvas. The bottom line is that nothing occurs in creation without some "I" in the Fabric of Consciousness (otherwise known as God with a big

"G") willing it. In other words, no matter how complex and random an event, or an outcome, on the Canvas, some monad, some body, or some group, *is always responsible*.[36]

Before moving on, let me add this one final tidbit to our discussion of this new dimension by informing you that the amount of chance (i.e., the amount of a dimension) in creation is not a constant. The amount of chance in the universe (or in a local grouping) grows and shrinks with (among other things) the number of interested and engaged monads. This truth is moderately important for you to know because it has many practical implications, so let us pause and explore it a bit.

Let us start by reminding ourselves that when there is only one monad, when it is only "I" working on creation, there is no chance. We already know this. In the beginning when it is just God, there is nothing to interfere with the intent of a single monad, and so creation is instant and literal. That changes when you add more monads. As soon as you have even two, the possibility of random interference exists. Practically it won't happen right away because the Canvas of Creation is infinite, and with only a few monads, it is easy to

---

[36] So does this mean that accidents never occur and that all things happen for a reason? Absolutely not. Accidents happen, for reasons of greed, stupidity, lack of focus, all the time, especially on this, as yet, Blindfolded planet. If somebody gets drunk, gets in a car, and kills you dead, that's not the willful result of creative intent, that's the unfortunate outcome of the act of selfish and childish stupidity. Accidents happen all the time and so, word to the wise, be alert, pay attention, and play safe.

avoid interference, and easy to co-ordinate between independent wills if that becomes a necessity. Indeed, even when there are twelve painters in the room, there would only be a few (if any) chance occurrences. With only two or twelve there is lots of space but, more the point, communication is easy between only two or twelve. With only two or twelve, we pretty much always know what the other is going to do just as soon as they know what they are going to do. We are all connected in the Fabric, after all, and *our* thoughts are always *our* thoughts. With twelve it is always easy to follow what is happening in the Fabric, and what is going on in creation and so chance doesn't occur–even though the potential for it is there. However, add 1,700 painters to the same room and the probability of chance occurrences goes up dramatically. With this many monads painting in the same room, chance events begin to happen, not all the time, but enough to make you wonder. Obviously as we add more painters (i.e., monads), the probability of a chance event occurring rises until we reach the "popping point" and chance begins to happen all the time. We can define the popping point formally as:

The Popping Point

> The point where a quantitative addition of number leads to the qualitative emergence of dimension.

At that point, the dimension emerges fully into consciousness. At what point a dimension like chance "pops" isn't so important as is the idea that the amount of the dimension that exists *increases* with the number of monads! The creative principle is easy enough to state. Dimensions in creation are quantitatively dependent on the number of monads in the Fabric of Consciousness at any given time. This whole principle (i.e., that chance increases with the number of monads in creation) is important enough to express in a creative formula.

Chance

$$T^{otal}Chance = fnMonads$$

The formula reads, "The total amount of chance in creation is a function of the number of monads working on creation." The more monads you add, the more chance you will get.[37]

---

[37] It is important to note here that the amount of chance in creation is dependent on additional factors. For example, how "close" monads are to each other as they work together will have an impact on the number of random events that occur. Many monads all working in close quarters with each other will necessarily interfere with each other's creative intent, thereby increasing the amount of "chance" in the local area of creation they work in. Similarly, certain "styles" of creation can also increase the amount of chance. Monads who are careful and considerate, who don't like to "splash" paint on the Canvas, will necessarily have less impact on the creation of others than those who create with more gusto. And note that the reverse is also true. Many monads working together can *decrease* chance and *increase* creative coordinating and efficiency. If we all focus on the same thing, the same outcome, the same creative

Now I know some of you may be put off by formulas, but don't be. Stating this in formula form is useful for the same reason that stating the relationship between consciousness and energy in "law" form was useful. It is simply a reminder of an important creative principle. Anybody thinking about doing anything more than basic creation needs to be able to remember these important laws, principles, and relationships and apply them in their creative practice. The bottom line is we enhance our power when we know, understand, and play by the rules. These formulas and laws can help organize our thinking and make us more powerful creators. Put another way, you will get a lot farther along in manifesting the things you want if you understand the way creation works. When you understand how it works, the rules work for you. If you don't understand the principles, you won't always get what you want, and even if you do it might take you longer, and

---

vision, things happen with more efficiency, less random outcome, and more creative brilliance. This ability to co-ordinate and synergize creative efforts when we work together as a *collective* is alluded to in the Bible in Mathew 18:19 "Again, truly I tell you that if two of you on earth agree about anything they ask for, it will be done for them by my Father in heaven." If you replace "Father in heaven" with the Fabric of Consciousness then you can see the relevance of the passage immediately. As an important side note, any big creative "shifts" that we might want to undertake will depend, in very great measure, on the ability of monads to come together on the Canvas with the same vision, and same intent. Hence the significance of the work on archetypes you will do at the LP Intermediate level of study.

prove a more frustrating experience. Remember, our goal is fun and not work so anything that we can do to reduce the work in creation is always welcomed.

Now, those of you with a theological background, or those trained in the so called "mystery" schools, might want to nod to yourselves knowingly at this point and think that the introduction of the dimension of chance has introduced the possibility of the *degradation of creation* (or something like that). You might want to think that with the introduction of chance there is now the possibility that we (and by "we" I mean Immortal Spirit) could lose control of things. You might want to think that with the chance factor, we have introduced the possibility of chaos (i.e., uncontrolled manifestation) or even evil. What happens when we are dealing with billions of monads instead of only thousands? Will it be possible to control the random manifestations, or will creation just begin to boil in an uncontrollable and descending creative soup?

And what would we do if creation descended?

Would it become dangerous to let everybody do their own thing?

Would individual wills lead to collective chaos?

Would we need to take steps?

Would we need some sort of "executive authority" in order to manage manifestation and prevent the chaos?

Would some "boss guy" (or several boss guys in an ascending hierarchy) need to institute "rules" that everyone would follow in order to ensure that things did not spiral out of control?

Would we need laws, commandments, and such to prevent an "evil" descent into chaos?

It's a good set of questions, and I don't mean to dismiss them. To be honest, I can see there is a certain logic to this line of thinking, especially when considered against the backdrop of this world. Given the way things are here, I can see where this kind of idea would be appealing on so many different levels. I mean, there is this dimension of chance after all and the more monads who have "the power", the more chance there will be, and the more likely it would be to spiral out of control.

Right?

Wrong!

I agree, it is not a totally unreasonable line of thinking and, given the conditions on this earth and the job you came to do, you can be *forgiven* for thinking this way. However you must know it is not true, and if you think like that it is past time to put that kind of thinking aside.

Creation doesn't work like that.

We are all much, much, much more competent than that sort of thinking gives us credit for. We are loving, compassionate, connected, and aware, as is the nature of consciousness. We have been "around the block" (i.e. have incarnated in a body) thousands of times and are by now experts at creation. We have been doing it for eons (despite the fact that we don't remember while we wear the Blindfold[38]). We know how to get what we want and we know how to have fun doing it.

We are experts and we know exactly what we are doing.

We do not need laws and commandments.

We do not need punishments and damnations.

And besides, that kind of thinking is based on a huge false premise. Just because chance has been introduced into the equation does not mean that there is any possibility that we would ever lose control. This kind of thinking is totally incomprehensible when you keep in mind the primary Truth of creation which is that energy is merely a dream inside the mind of God. Creation is just a thought and as such, God (I/we) has total control over it. If God (I/we) ever, and I do mean ever, dreamt something not good in any way, if things occurred that were not enjoyable by any standard, if chaos threatened to run out of control in even the slightest manner, if the dream became a nightmare and nobody wanted it to go on any more, we would either change the dream and wait for reality to change, or we would stop dreaming and the dream would go away, *poof*, like magic.

Energy follows intent, and if there is no intent, there is no manifestation.

The bottom line is, creation (of any kind) requires constant attention and if we don't give it attention, it languishes and

---

[38] See Michael Sharp, Parable of the Blindfold.

dies.[39]

It is that simple.

However, before we get too positive about the emergence of chance, we do have to deal with one other possibility that some of your world philosophies and religions like to offer to try and preserve the notion of chaos, evil, degradation, etc.

Consider this example.

Suppose, for the moment, that some individual monad, some

---

[39] You can, of course, see this in children who require constant attention from their parents in order to survive and thrive. And this doesn't mean a few minutes in the morning and a little bit at night. It does not mean quality time once a week or once a month. It means constant physical, emotional, and intellectual attention. I know it seems like a big commitment, but did anyone ever say raising a child was easy?

Our societies, and especially our western societies, are extremely hostile to children. We shuffle our children off "to play" or to daycare and to school the instant they are able to go. We box ourselves in and provide little space for them. We are too busy playing adult games, working, taking care of our commitments to others, making money, buying cars, and so on to really pay them the attention they require. In the worst cases our children get quality attention once a month or less and often from only one parent. You can imagine the emotional problems that can accumulate over a decade or two of that kind of treatment.

If we want our children to grow up with healthy minds, connected to spirit, this will have to change. Our beliefs and values will have to change and our societies will have to change to support increased attention from both parents. I know it is a lot of change especially considering how little attention we now give to our children, but, it will be done. The (crystal) children will demand it.

"bad seed", doesn't like the orderly unfolding of creation. Suppose some monad decides he is bored with all the fancy palaces and lush gardens that others like to create. Suppose this one would rather see everything as an ugly and chaotic mess, where discord, pain, and suffering rule the day. Suppose some "chaotic soul" thinks that all that happiness, fun, and play in creation is stupid and idiotic. Suppose, perhaps out of ennui and boredom, some dark satanic light emerges that actually takes pleasure out of chaos and disintegration.

Suppose this one has thoughts that a spiral into darkness might be fun to watch.

Suppose this one started to recruit others to the nefarious plan and suppose, at some point, they start to create chaos?

Suppose that after a while the chaos and darkness started to bleed into other areas of the canvas.

Suppose the ones creating the chaos and darkness were asked, pretty please, to stop.

Suppose they didn't.

Suppose they went ahead anyway and started to darken and corrupt the Canvas wherever they could.

Suppose this pissed everyone off.

Suppose they "fell" from grace.

Suppose they were thrown out of the Garden.

Suppose that, after being ejected from the Garden, they became hurt, angered, and embittered by the rejection.

Suppose then that out of hurt and anger the leader of the monadic outcast group decided to set up his own corner of creation where fire, brimstone, suffering, and pain were the name of the game?

Suppose that this one, out of a malicious sense of vengeance, decided to start "tricking" other monads, the ones who had shunned him and his group, to come join him in the flames?

Suppose that the other monads were too stupid and disconnected to know the difference?

Suppose that a decision in that direction was considered an unforgivable sin, and that once condemned no amount of begging and pleading would ever get them back into the Garden?

Suppose that other monads were not powerful enough to leave the flames, and suppose that even if they did they would be stopped at the Pearly Gates and rejected by their brothers and sisters in the Fabric?

I suppose it is possible that something like this could be created.

I suppose it is possible that some monad, out of some twisted sense of shame and revenge, would develop some twisted sense of creation and then try and lead others into that twisted view.

I suppose it is possible that some anti-creator might even succeed in getting enough souls on his side to overwhelm the crystalline order of the universe.

I suppose because, when you think about it, anything is

possible. Creation is just a dream inside the mind of "I" and within that dream there are no limits, except the limit of imagination. And so a universe of pain, suffering, and chaos is possible, if imaginable. But then, just because it is possible does not mean anybody would want to imagine it, or that anybody is stupid enough, or twisted enough, or insensitive enough, to create it. In fact, the whole line of reasons that leads to the presentation of chaos, fire, and brimstone as a plausible reality in the Fabric is, given the nature of the Fabric of Consciousness, beyond plausible.

We are all connected in the Fabric.

We are all loving and compassionate.

We are all conscious and aware.

Most important, we are all part of the same monadic tapestry. For one to do these things to other, with premeditated intensity, would be unthinkable and absurd.

It would be like your right hand picking up a hammer and smashing its own body into a pulp.

It would be like your left hand mutilating and cutting off your right hand just because the left didn't like what the right was doing.

It is possible to imagine, but it is absurd to think such a thing would unfold.

And if it did then it would be nothing short of neurotic pathology.

And let me assure you, the glorious Fabric of Consciousness is about as far away from neurotic pathology as you can possibly get.

Of course, this is not to say that a collective preference for extra chance and chaos does not operate. There are areas of Creation where some monads like to play with the potential of *chaos*. These get together in large groups and dance and gyrate in the froth of their own randomness. They find the extra deviation, variation, and chaos interesting and fun. And of course, it can be fun, either as a short-term experience or as a long-term commitment. But to say that such an interest in the deviation and variation of a little extra chaos is somehow against the will of a single monad, to say that such a thing is evil or bad, to say eternal banishment, or cosmic levels of pain and suffering, should result, is to present yourself as someone totally disconnected and out of touch with the loving, compassionate, aware, blissful, and powerful nature of the Fabric.

Creation is not a one-size–fits-all sort of thing. Variation and deviation of all forms are accepted, and even encouraged, as nothing more nor less than the joyful avoidance of ennui and boredom. The only rule that is involved, the only thing that guides our direction and confines our choices, is the stipulation that you not impose your will, interfere with another, or otherwise hurt and destroy where you are not welcome and where you do not have explicit permission. Respect the wishes of others, keep your distance when asked, and do the things that interest and impassion you only in the context of respectful, compassionate, and aware co-creation.

In short, don't be a dick-head.

Make sure everyone involved is having fun.

I'd call this the golden rule: Do unto others as you would have them do unto you. In fact this rule, this stipulation that you not impose, interfere, or hurt, goes much farther than even that by making the reference point not the individual preferences of "I" but the personal preferences of "you," the primary point of judgment. I might like something, but you might not, and if you don't, then I have no right to impose, interfere, or otherwise upset your little corner of creation. In fact, it is quite the opposite. If I am going to paint on your canvas then I have a deeply seated responsibility to improve, in a direction that is totally satisfying to you, your creative efforts. And while this might seem like a lot to ask, in reality it is not. We are all part of the same Fabric of Consciousness and this sort of consideration comes naturally. We naturally respect others, we naturally pay attention to our creation, and we naturally show compassion and consideration. It is in our very nature.[40]

---

[40] At this point some readers may be looking out at the world on Earth and saying to themselves, "Yeah, right." The greed, graft, suffering, violence and woe on this earth, the way one person consciously (or unconsciously) interferes, exploits, and harms another, would seem to belie these positive statements about our true spiritual nature and instead put the evidential weight down on the absurd notions of chaos and evil outlined earlier. It is a bit of a philosophical problem, of course, and one that priests, pundits, and hierophants have tried, over the centuries, to solve. Thankfully there is an explanation for what happens on this Earth that does not violate statements about the nature of consciousness as loving, compassionate, connected, blissful, and aware provided at the outset of this treatise. That explanation involves a Blindfold, a creative mission, a Great Work, and a Sacrifice. That story is told in several

We Are the Glorious Throng of Elohim

And that brings our discussion of the dimension of chance to a close. You now know everything you need to know (for this book at least) about the dimension of chance. You know that chance is a dimension that emerged in creation when there was more than one monad. You know that the dimension did not become significant or noticeable until there were thousands of monads painting on the Canvas. You know that the amount of chance in creation is variable. You know chance added a significant new factor to our creative equation that was going to guarantee all sorts of new fun and excitement. You also know what comes next in our story of creation. You know that after we had identified and processed the new dimension so we understood it in consciousness, we got down to play. And of course, with all 1,743 monads at the four levels of creation, and with the amazing and wonderful new element of chance in creation, I can tell you, it was a lot of fun.

It was amazing.

It was wonder.

It was bliss.

It was joy!

---

places on the Lightning Path including *The Song of Creation: The Story of Genesis, The Book of Life: Ascension and the Divine World Order,* and also in the archetypes and imagery of the Halo/Sharp archetype system. These resources are all part of the *LP Intermediate A* level of study. Visit http://www.thelightningpath.com/ for more information.

But even more than these it was fascinating, in the intellectual sense of the word. The element of chance really did enhance our creative play and gave us a whole new world of possibility that delighted, titillated, and challenged us. But, of course, it could not last forever.

It would have to stop somewhere.

At some point "the inevitable" had to happen.

But not to worry because when the boredom set in, we knew what to do. We would say "LET THERE BE MORE LIGHTS," we would add another level to our pyramid, and we would redo creation anew. The only question that we all had at the end of the fourth level of the Unfolding was what the new number was going to be. How many more little ones would we add at the new level of creation?

1

2

12

1,728

???????

Well, to make a long story a bit shorter, at the point where we got bored with the permutations and combinations of 1,743, at the point where chance no longer proved sufficient to stave off boredom, and at the point where we declared *let there be more lights,* we added exactly 5,159,780,352 new monads to the

Fabric of Consciousness.[41]

Visualized in pyramid form, the new pyramid would look like this.

1

2

12

1,728

5,159,780,352

It is an impressive number. And I suppose at this point you are wondering why this number. Well, the issues here are largely identical to the issues at the previous level. That is, our primary concern was to add enough new monads to provide a quantum leap forward. We wanted to provide ourselves with sufficient challenge to ensure boredom didn't creep back into the equation. I am sure you will agree, adding five billion certainly qualifies as a quantum leap.

But why five billion?

Would not have one billion or even one million have provided a quantum leap from 1,700? The answer to that is, yes they would have.

It is true.

We could have picked a different number, but we didn't. Instead what we did was decide to stick with a tradition that

---

[41] Giving us a total of 5,159,782,095 monads in creation.

we had started at the previous level. Recall that at the last stage of the Unfolding (i.e., in the jump from twelve to 1,728) we used a particular formulation to derive our new number. We took the number of little ones at the bottom level of the pyramid (which in the previous case was twelve at the third level) and we cubed that number. We chose our new number for the fourth level of creation by raising the number twelve (the number of Little Ones) to the power of three. Those of you who hate numbers might find this a little obtuse and technical but it is not that hard to understand if we take it step by step.

First of all, let us lay out the three first levels of creation in our "I" Pyramid as we did earlier. At the fourth level of creation our pyramid looks like this:

I

II

I	I	I	I	I	I	I	I	I	I
144	144	144	144	144	144	144	144	144	144

Recall that we got our fourth level by cubing the previous level. That is we took the total number of little ones at the third level (i.e., twelve) and put twelve times twelve (12x12) little ones down as the new level of creation. This allowed us to insert a symmetrical and elegant 12x12 underneath each "I" of the previous level.

I

II

I   I   I   I   I   I   I   I   I   I

12x12 12x12 12x12 12x12 12x12 12x12 12x12 12x12 12x12 12x12

We can summarize this structure as we did before by adding it all up like this.

Based on the fact that our decision to cube the little ones worked out so well (i.e. not only did it add deviation and variation, but it also added the dimension of chance), we decided that we'd do the same thing in transition from the fourth level to the fifth level of the Unfolding. That is, we would take the previous number of little ones, cube that, and instantiate that number of new I's at the new bottom level of the Unfolding. Since at this point this would be the second time we did this, and since we would likely do it again in the future, we could summarize this new tradition in a formula thusly.

The Tradition

$$T_{newlevel} = N_{littleones}^{3}$$

The formula would read like this. The total number of new monads (T) that we will add for the next level of the Unfolding is equal to the current number of Little Ones (N) (i.e., monads at the bottom level) cubed.

Simple, elegant, and easy to apply.

135

In the case of our transition from level three to level four, the numbers look like this.

$$T_{newlevel} = N_{littleones}{}^3$$
or
$$T_{newlevel} = 12^3$$
or
$$T = 1,728$$

In the case of the transition from the fourth to the fifth level, the numbers look like this.

$$T_{newlevel} = N_{littleones}{}^3$$
or
$$T_{newlevel} = 1,728^3$$
or
$$T = 5,159,780,352$$

This would give us a pyramid of I that looked like this.

1
2
12
1,728
5,159,780,352

It is an impressive number and a definite quantum leap forward. And of course, you know what happens next. We instantiate the new monads and start all over again. And as always it was amazing and blissful and joyful. However, just as in the previous level we did not get too far along the path of our new creation before we noticed that something was different about the way creation was working. Something had changed about the way intention was translating into manifestation.

Once again, as with the introduction of the dimension of chance at the previous level, energy was not responding as we expected it to. Something was up and fortunately, this time, it did not take us by surprise.

This time we almost expected it.

This time we realized right away what had happened. At the fifth level of creation, when energy stopped responding to intent as expected, we knew a new dimension, a new sephiroth, had once again popped into existence.

The Dawn of Time

Interestingly enough, you already know the name of the new dimension that popped at the fifth level by the interchangeable names of *inertia* or *time*. I realize you may be scratching your head here wondering how the heck adding monads to the Fabric of Consciousness creates the dimension of time (or inertia), but rest assured it is not so difficult to understand. However, understanding it will require a bit of background in order to tease out some of the more important implications. Let us start out by introducing (or re-introducing if you have read The Book of Life: *Ascension and the Divine World Order*) an important concept called the creative moment. In that book I define a creative moment as the time it takes to manifest a particular intent. From The Book of Life:

> What do we mean by the idea of a creative moment? For us as Immortal Spirit, a moment is simply the time it takes to manifest intent. We have "moments" in physicality that are exactly the same as Spiritual moments though we are not normally aware of them as we are usually absorbed in the illusion of linear time. While in physicality, a moment is distinguished by the cycles that bring our intent into physical existence. A moment begins when we express our intent and ends when that intent is realized to one extent or another.
>
> You can think of this in terms of the normal daily activity of making breakfast. When you wake up and you decide (intend) to make breakfast, you enter into your breakfast moment. You grab the bacon, turn on the stove, scramble the eggs, grate the cheese, pour the milk, and make the coffee. When you are finished the process of making breakfast and finished the process of consumption you have completed your breakfast moment. Notice here that you undertake many other activities on your way to manifesting your breakfast. Each of these other activities also represents a moment for you. When you grate cheese, you are having a cheesy moment. When you scramble the eggs, you are having a

scrambled moment. If you pause to go to the washroom, you have a bathroom moment (or movement as the case may be).

Thus a creative moment is simply the time it takes to manifest a specific intent.

Now, recall the third law of creation.

Energy responds to intent instantly and literally

The third law states that *energy follows intent instantly and literally*. No problems there. With this law in mind, we may define the creative moment as simply the span from appearance of an idea in consciousness to its manifestation in energy. That is, a creative moment is the span between thought and manifestation.

The Creative Moment

Creative Moment =
Span from thought to manifestation

In the beginning, and as indicated by the third law of creation, the span from thought to manifestation is flat. That is, there is no gap between idea and creation. You already know this and you already know why this is. Energy is a reflection of the consciousness of God. Energy is consciousness, consciousness is God, and because of this direct internal *relationship*, energy is always an immediate reflection of that consciousness.

The Relationship

> energy = consciousness
> **= God =**
> consciousness = energy

Thus, in the beginning, a creative moment is instant.[42] If I

---

[42] You should be aware that even in the beginning creation didn't just appear all at once. Creation emanates and expands as part of the process of play, and this emanation is spread out, like an expanding balloon, over a subset of our eternities. The point that I'm making here with the creative moment isn't that duration doesn't exist in the beginning but that there is no break between what is in consciousness and what is reflected in the energy. Intent is manifested instantly (and this would be the flat creative moment) but our creation can be held in consciousness for extended periods. That is duration. In this context, it is important to distinguish between duration and time. Duration is a measure of the length of the existence of a creation. If I hold an idea in my mind of a square box, that box is "in duration" as long as I hold the idea. In terms of consciousness, duration cannot really be measured. It is just an internal sense of being involved in something (i.e., involved in the creative moment) for a certain span of consciousness intent. On the other hand, time is, as we shall see, different than duration and although they tend to become inseparably intertwined in practice, it is theoretically useful to keep the idea of them separate. Time is a

think something, energy, because it is just another aspect of consciousness, immediately reflects that change. Of course, this relationship changed a bit at the fourth level. That is because at the fourth level the dimension of chance popped into existence. With chance operating, it was no longer possible to assume that intent would manifest literally and so the *literal* aspect of manifestation (i.e., the second part of the third law that states that manifestation is literal) began to break down.[43]

Interestingly, the same sort of thing happens at the fifth level of creation. At the fifth level, consciousness and energy changed even more because at the fifth level of creation the monads in the Fabric noticed a delay between thought and manifestation. That is, at the fifth level a monad could intend a result, but that result no longer appeared instantly (or literally) in creation.

Now pause for a moment and consider this.

Given the nature of energy and its relationship to God, it

---

measure of how long it takes to manifest an idea. Duration is a measure of the length of physical manifestation (i.e., the universe).

[43] Once again this breakdown was practical, not technical. Technically the relationship still held since technically everything happening on the Canvas was the literal result of some monad's intent. Practically however it was no longer the case since accidental impositions, splashes and drips of paint that interfered with and modified creation in unexpected ways were occurring (and would occur with increasing frequency as more monads were added to the Canvas).

should seem inconceivable that there should ever be any sort of delay in manifestation. Energy is a reflection of consciousness; energy *is* consciousness, so to suggest that a delay could emerge is to undermine the fundamental truth of the relationship between energy and consciousness, and to call into question the identity of reality and consciousness is to put a wall between consciousness and energy that simply cannot exist.

So why then, at the fifth level of the Unfolding, do we begin to notice a delay?

Why does there seem to be a disconnect between intent and manifestation?

Why, at the fifth level of the Unfolding, does this new factor in the equation, this new dimension in creation, this "time" delay, pop into existence?

Well, as it turns out, it is not that hard to understand. That is, there is a rational explanation for this apparent total collapse of the foundation of Creation (i.e., the three laws), but getting to that explanation requires a little bit of thought. First, we had to realize that even though a delay in manifestation was emerging at the fifth level of the Unfolding, the third law was not being violated at all. Even with an apparent delay between thought and manifestation, energy was still following intent in an instant and literal fashion. Technically, everything was as it should be and the three laws were in operation. However, in practical terms it was a different story. The difference arises from the fact that with that many monads working in creation (i.e., five billion plus) there are often many individual monads interested in a single creative phenomenon. A single creative idea, for example, the manifestation of a blue crystal palace, could be *shared* among hundreds, thousands, or even millions of monads. Having millions interested in a creative idea is quite a leap forward from 1,700, and it makes a significant difference. What happens is that when you get a lot of monads working on the same idea, in the same corner of the Canvas, the link between the (now collective) will of all interested monads and the manifestation of that will is no longer direct.

The basic problem is in the combination of intent, and how energy responds to multiple requests at once. I know it sounds complicated, but it is not, and an example will help clear this up. Imagine for a moment that there are a million monads working on a single creative task. Let us call our million monads the *Group*. The Group has decided (for various reasons known only to the individual members) to get together and create a blue crystal city somewhere in the energy stream. They are all excited about the idea of collectively exploring the possibility of the blue castle so, as soon as they are together, they begin intending their creation. They all agree on the basic form and they manifest that and thus it does not take long for them to create a beautiful blue crystal palace. They create walls and spires, towers and gardens that are absolutely magnificent to behold. When they are done, they go and play with the castle.

The play goes on for a while without much change. Everybody is having so much fun that nobody thinks to alter the basic characteristics of the blue palace. There are small modifications as gardens and towers come and go but by and large everyone sticks to the main plan and nobody gets too far out of line. However, and as you might expect, the utopian agreement cannot go on forever and at some point somebody will get impatient with the collective manifestation. It has to happen. Even with the combined creative genius of a million monads, all possibilities are eventually explored and when that happens, the blue crystal palace becomes a bore.

Let us imagine now that one individual monad, let us call her Sparkle, does indeed get bored. She is tired of the ho-hum of the blue crystal palace and wants to get over the boredom as quickly as possible. She thinks about it for a moment and gets the idea to intend a huge splash of red someplace in the middle of the blue crystal castle. Sparkle thinks this is a grand idea. Not only will it add spectacular contrast to the blue crystal structures but it will also shake everyone up.[44] And besides, the Group had been getting a little complacent and the new manifestation will help bring some of the spice of creation back into their game. So Sparkle, who is getting quite excited thinking about the implications, turns her attention to the energy and immediately visualizes a huge and expanding splash of red deep within the crystal structure. She goes for the biggest, brightest, and most garish red she can think of in the hopes of really opening things up and jarring the Group into an expanded awareness of their own boredom. She intends the red and immediately stands back to enjoy the explosion.

---

[44] And, as every trickster Spirit knows, shaking things up once in a while is a good thing.

Unfortunately, Sparkle is hugely disappointed when, for all her conscious effort, the only thing that appears is a little dot of red in the middle of the big blue palace. Sparkle is quite surprised by this (as you can imagine) and she immediately exclaims, "What the heck is going on here? I intended a huge splash of red but only a small dot appeared".

"Doesn't this violate the first law that there shall be no limits on creation?" she says.

"Doesn't this violate the second law that energy will always follow the contours of consciousness?" she wonders.

"Doesn't this violate the third law that manifestation shall always be an instant mirror of the creator's consciousness?" she exclaims.

"The Foundations are crumbling," she cries.

"The Relationship is void," she despairs.[45]

And you have to admit it certainly appears that something is fundamentally wrong. However, although it seems like things are falling apart, they really are not. The fact that Sparkle isn't getting an instant manifestation of her idea has nothing to do with the three rules of energy manifestation (which are still in proper technical operation), or the Relationship, or the Foundation, and everything to do with the fact that Sparkle is now working as part of a larger group of identically interested

---

[45] Remember the Relationship is that
God=Consciousness=Energy=Creation=Energy=Consciousness=God.
In other words, it is all related.

monads.

That is, it is *the Group* that is the cause of the delay, and not a breakdown in the Relationship, or the Foundation.

It works like this.

Even though Sparkle wants a splash of red, initially, nobody else in the Group does. While Sparkle gets her big idea to splash red, everyone else is still intending blue. What happens here is the intentional impact of these 999,999 blue thinking monads, locked as they are in their old patterns of creation, dramatically reduces the effectiveness of Sparkle's idea. Remember the second law here, energy responds to intent. Intent here includes the intent of Sparkle *and* the intent of the Group and so when you consider manifestation you must consider the intent of everyone involved. Because of the relationship between energy and consciousness, any monad with an interest in any corner of creation becomes an automatic *influence* on that corner of creation.

This is very important, so make sure you understand.

Take a spot on the Canvas of creation and pay any kind of attention to it and you are having an influence on that creative space. The influence might be terribly small, but that doesn't matter here. What is important for you to understand is that if you, or ten others, or a billion others, pay conscious attention to something on the Canvas, if you take an interest, you make yourself an influence. Given this new collective wrinkle in the Foundation of Creation, we might revise our second law to include this idea of a collective creation. Thus at the fifth level of creation and beyond we restate the second law of creation thusly:

146

The Second Law Revised

> Energy follows the intent of all interested monads

As you can see, this is not that hard to understand. Energy is still following the intent of consciousness, but now the response of the energy is complicated by the fact that many monads are working on the Canvas and their collective intent is thus influencing, more or less, the direction of creative flow.

The question now becomes, how much "more" or "less" is the influence.

It is important.

In the early stages of the Unfolding you can rely on the three laws to give you instant and literal gratification of your creative desires. However, past a certain point that instant and literal gratification is no longer always possible. This isn't really a problem, since ultimately this adds a new wrinkle to creation, a new factor to the equation, a new *dimension* in creation, and this is good because this brings deviation, variation, and interest. However it can become a problem especially when monads fail to recognize the new *reality* and the new challenges that emerge. If monads are not aware of the modification of the second law, and the new wrinkle in creation, monads (used to getting what they want exactly when they want it) can get frustrated and angry as a result. I tell you truly, no monad in creation wants to experience frustration and anger, and so all monads need to understand this new dimension if they want to continue to joyfully manifest on the Canvas of creation.

Thankfully, there is not that much to understand. Really there are only two things that you have to wrap your head around. One is the reality of the delay, and two is the extent of the delay. As far as the reality of the delay goes, you already know that with a lot of new monads working on the Canvas, manifestation of intent is delayed. As far as the extent of the delay goes, that depends entirely on three factors: attention, focus, and the number of monads interested and paying attention. All other things being equal, the more *attention* you pay to a creative intent, and the more *focus* you bring to your attention, the more powerful your intent will be, the more influence you will have on the Canvas, and the more likely your intent will manifest with only minimal delay. On the other hand, the more monads that are arrayed against you, the more monads intending a different thing, the more monads paying attention to your creative corner of the Canvas, the more influence and impact they have. If one thousand monads focus on the same thing, and intend the same outcome, their attention and focus will summate and provide a very powerful impact on the Canvas. By contrast, if only one monad is focusing on a particular outcome, their intent will be less powerful than the one thousand. If you put the one against the one thousand then obviously the one is at a major disadvantage. If the one gets what he wants at all it will only be after significant delay, and only after major attention and focus is brought to bear.

Summarizing, we might say that the intent of the many (which we shall henceforth call the *mass consciousness*) has a tendency to average out, or even cancel out, the intent of the few (or the one). In other words mass consciousness tends to lock creation into patterns that are resistant to change.[46]

That this happens in creation can be very frustrating, as Sparkle finds out. When she tries to get her red splash, the intent of 999,999 blue thinkers waters down the splash of red and leaves Sparkle's brilliant idea a shadow of its original glory. The sad bottom line for die-hard individualists is that as long as most people in the Group intend blue, poor little Sparkle is going to be disappointed in her desire to see red, and that is just the way it is, not because Sparkle's ideas are not important, and not because she is someone less powerful, capable, or divine than any of the others, but simply because she is intending alone, and in isolation, and as a result her intent is weighted down by the intent of others.

Interestingly enough, we earth people have a name for this resistance to manifestation that we experience in grouped creation. We call it *inertia*. As you can now see, inertia (from the perspective of Spirit) is nothing more than the averaging

---

[46] Of course, it is important to note that mass consciousness doesn't really exist. There is no "thing" out there (institutional or otherwise) that exists over and above the consciousness of the individual monad. Mass Consciousness is simply an emergent phenomenon, rooted in the individual intent of individual monads. Nevertheless and despite its status as mere illusion or emergent phenomenon, it (i.e. mass consciousness) has real and powerful consequences, as anybody who has ever tried to change anything will be able to attest to.

out of intent caused by the mass consciousness of interested monads.

> Inertia = resistance to manifestation experienced by monads as a result of the mass consciousness of grouped (i.e. interested) monads

Now, as you can probably guess, as consciousness continues to unfold, as more and more monads are added to the Fabric, there is going to be growing inertia in creation. More and more monads will tend to get wrapped up in "their thing," and their collective will (made more or less powerful by the attention and focus they present) creates a powerful inertia that will increase as the number of monads increases. We can write the relationship between the *new dimension* of inertia, and the number of monads in creation, as a formula

Inertia

> Inertia = fNMonads

The formula reads, the amount of inertia in creation is a function of the number of (interested and involved) monads.

Now keep in mind there is nothing Machiavellian here. It is just the way it is. We get locked into our creative ruts and absorbed in the enjoyment of our creation. While we are lost in the moment we necessarily create resistance to new ideas because our focus is on what is, and what we are doing, and not what others might be intending. Please understand here, this is not necessarily an active resistance (though it could be). Sparkle doesn't come up to the blue monads and find a bunch of stubborn old souls saying this is the way to do things so bugger off. Monads are all part of the Fabric, all part of the collective consciousness of creation, and all part of the same family. The default is to consider, help, and encourage. Thus new ideas are not normally resisted because monads do not want to try them out. Resistance is simply the natural outcome of group creation. More accurately, it is the technical outcome of multi-monadal manifestation. Energy responds to intent literally and instantly at all times, but when there is a lot of intent focused on a certain idea (like the manifestation of a blue crystal palace), the collective mind imposes "tradition," and inertia is experienced in the energy.

To summarize then, the three laws (i.e., The Foundation of creation) are still in proper technical operation but when there is more than one monad working on the same idea, a technical averaging occurs that causes a delay in manifestation that we call inertia. The amount of inertia experienced in a particular corner of the Canvas is a direct function of the number of interested monads.

There is a lot more I could say about the technical details of inertia, how groups work, the importance of attention and focus, and all that jazz, but I will leave these more technical discussions for later. For now, just be careful not to take the idea of creative inertia too far. The fact that there is inertia in creation, and the fact that this will increase as we add more monads, does not mean that Sparkle is doomed to a universe of blue crystal palaces. Even as an individual, creating what we want does not become impossible in a group context. It just requires a little more effort. If we want red, we can have red, but we will have to do the legwork. We will have to "fight" for it, not in the literal sense of harming another just to force our way, but in the figurative sense of tapping, poking, pushing, and prodding so we can get others' attention.

We need to *get our idea out there* and we need to convince others that it is a good thing.

We need to get "local stakeholders" (i.e. monads working on our corner of the Canvas) on board.

We need, in short, to convince enough monads in the Group that the new idea for the splash of red deserves consideration, and that they should help, or at least back off long enough to allow it to occur. It is not necessarily that hard, and we do not even need a majority. We really only need monads in the local area to give way a bit, and a few interested monads helping out to get our red splash. However, the more collective buy-in we get, the more souls choose to try the splash, the more spectacular it will be.

Now, in order to help clarify all this, let us put ourselves back into Sparkle's shoes for a moment. Remember, she intended a red splash but only got a pathetic little dot. Now you see why. She is fighting inertia caused by the mass consciousness. You will also see at this point that there is a way around the disappointing result. However, she does have her work cut out for her. Getting her splash is not going to be easy because she is going to have to convince a lot of monads it is a good idea. Basically, she'll have to send her idea out into the mass consciousness and then demonstrate, practice, beg, and cajole to get enough monads interested and on board with her. It won't be impossible, but it will be work. At this point the *only* question that is relevant to Sparkle's creative endeavor here (and really the only question that is relevant to any creative endeavor when a group is involved) is whether or not Sparkle wants to put in the necessary effort. If she decides yes, and if she has the requisite motivation and determination, she will eventually get what she wants. She will get enough people on her side either actively helping with the red splash or just getting out of the way. How soon she gets her splash, and how big it is, will depend entirely on how efficiently Sparkle works, on how effectively she wakes monads up to the new idea, and how many monads she convinces to help. On the other hand, if she decides the red splash is not worth the effort, she will never overcome inertia and creation will continue on in blue forever and ever, or until such time as somebody else with enough interest, desire, motivation, and determination comes along.[47]

It really is that simple.

---

[47] As a side note, if you are a fan of The Secret, compare what you have just learned here about how to manifest in creation, and what the Law of Attraction teaches you. As you can hopefully now see, the popularized Law of Attraction is a grotesque, and in my opinion, useless and insulting (to your intelligence) simplification of creative laws and principles.

We started this section talking about time and inertia. At the outset I said that at the fifth level of creation the dimension of time popped into existence. I said the emergence of this dimension was not that hard to understand, but that a little background information would be needed. We now have that background information in place and we can now understand the nature of this new dimension of time. Before I provide a definition of time, however, let us once more consider the creative moment. Recall that when I introduced the topic above I said that the creative moment was simply the span between thought and manifestation. I noted that in the beginning the span was instant, but that this changed when we had groups of monads working on ideas. When groups get involved, a delay is introduced, inertia kicks in, and the creative moment is no longer instant. How "non-instant" the span will be will depend, among other things, on the amount of local *inertia*. We can visualize all this by drawing the creative moment as a bracketed line like so.

The Creative Moment

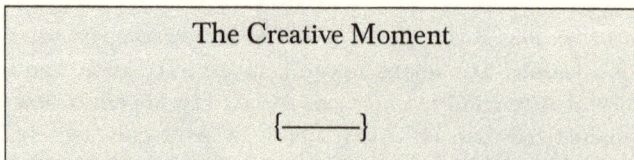

The Creative Moment

{———}

The bracket on the left of the line symbolizes the inception of the idea and the bracket on the right symbolizes its manifestation in energy. The line in between represents the *time* it takes to get from thought to manifestation. At this point we can finally say that the dimension of time is nothing more or less than the length of the line that spans between inception of thought and manifestation in energy.

Time

Time is the length of the line between inception
of an idea and its manifestation in energy

This is important and there are a host of implications, not the least of which is the fact that the amount of time it takes to do a task can be modified by altering factors in the collective consciousness. However, this is not the place to go into those. For now, consider this final technical tidbit: Not all creative moments are created equal. Depending on, among other things, the amount of inertia present at a specific location, a creative moment can be longer or shorter. We can illustrate this by drawing several lines of different length to illustrate the variable nature of the collective moment, and the amount of time that exists between thought and manifestation in each of these varying moments.

Instant creative moment
{}

```
Short creative moment
{——}

Longer creative moment
{—————————}

Longest creative moment
{———————————————}
```

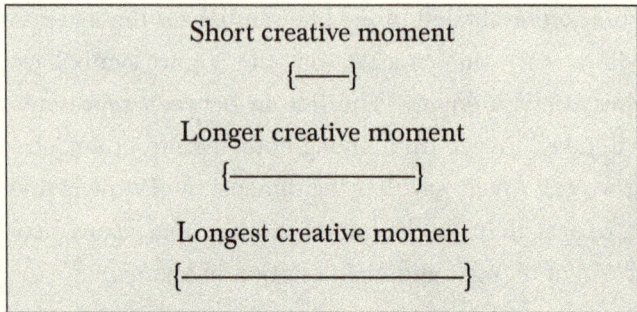

At this point in this accounting of the Unfolding of creation you now understand both random creative events, and time, and how these two new dimensions alter the practical reality of the three laws of creation. Before moving on I would like to place heavy emphasis on this new dimension of time. Indeed, it is hard to overestimate the importance of this addition to our creative endeavors. With the addition of the dimension of time we take a quantum leap forward in our technique of creative manifestation. With inertia and time in play we could, for example, *create permanency of form* where before we could not. Before the emergence of inertia and time, our creations were ephemeral and passing. Because of the nature of consciousness and energy, if we turned our attention from our creation, creation would dissipate immediately. Energy follows intent literally and instantly and without intent, creation crumbles. But this changes with time and inertia. With many millions of monads working on creation, there is intent to spare. In the new conditions at the fifth level of creation, we could now turn our attention away from our creations and they would still be there when we turned back.

Instead of creation disintegrating from lack of intent, it would *persist* beyond our individual gaze. The fact that so many others were with us in creation would give our creations *independence* from the individual.

This was a stunning development, and indeed changed the entire character of our creative endeavors. It brought new creative possibilities and would ensure deviation and variation for a long time to come. And so at the fifth level of creation, with 5,159,780,352 monads instantiated in the Fabric we, the throng of creation, started to play. And with five billion monads working in five levels of creation and creating with the dimensions of detail, perspective, chance, and time, things just kept getting more and more interesting. To say it was a lot of fun would be a gross understatement. In fact, I'm not sure there are words to describe how wonderful, exciting, and joyful creation was becoming as new dimensions kept popping into existence. But of course, in the end, it did not matter how spectacular the new dimension/sephiroth of time was, or how much opportunity for creative exploration we could find with it, in the end it had to end.

When you have an eternity of eternities to play in, everything eventually gets boring. It is the nature of consciousness. But, of course, there were no worries because we knew just what to do. When we get bored we simply add more monads to the Fabric using the formula:

$$T_{newlevel} = N_{littleones}^{3}$$

Doing so we would thus move from this...

1

2

12

1,728

5,159,780,352

...to this.

1

2

12

1,728

5,159,780,352

137,370,551,967,459,378,662,586,974,208

The only question for us at this new level of the Unfolding was not what the new number was going to be (we knew that already) but what the new dimension was going to be. Having gone through all this before, we were fairly certain that a new dimension would be added to creation at each level of the Unfolding. All we had to do was *play* to realize it.

All Spaced Out

And so, that is what we did. At the sixth level of creation, with more monads than we could possibility count, we got down to the serious business of play. And as it turns out, and as you might expect, "it" did happen again. At the sixth level of the Unfolding, a new dimension did emerge. Of course technically it didn't emerge fresh and new at the sixth level. As with the previous dimensions of time and chance, it had existed *in potential form* from the moment there was more than one monad intending in the Fabric. It was simply that up until the sixth level there was not enough of the dimension in existence for it to pop into awareness. This was not the case at the sixth level. At the sixth level of the Unfolding, there were more than enough monads in the Fabric to invoke the new dimension.

Perhaps you will not be surprised at this point to learn that the new dimension that emerged at the sixth level of creation was **space**. I would say that perhaps you are not surprised for a couple reasons. On the one hand, by now you are perhaps starting to remember these things on your own. Perhaps now these ancient, formerly veiled, Truths are no longer coming to you as strange and unknown, but as distantly familiar.

This is as it should be!

This is your birthright after all.

You are a monad, instantiated in the Fabric, and incarnated in the Body, and I am telling you nothing you do not already know deep down at the very core of your consciousness. However, for reasons explained in *The Book of Life: Ascension and the Divine World Order,* your connection with the Fabric has been severed, and your existence while incarnating on this Earth has been veiled. You were blindfolded, in short, and this blindfold you wear prevents you from seeing "the Truth and nothing but."[48] As you read through the words of this

---

[48] Read the Parable of the Blindfold.
http://www.thelightningpath.com/parables/parable-of-the-blindfold/

Book of Light, however, the blindfold begins to come off and you begin to see. Perhaps you do not see with the original clarity and force of your time outside the Body, and perhaps you are not open to full-blown mystical realizations just yet, but perhaps a flame deep inside has been awakened. If this is so, this is awesome, and your connection with these Truths should be encouraged. You can enhance your own connection by visualizing light streaming into the top of your skull, and by embracing with joy and playful wonder your growing understanding of the basic cosmological Truths of creation. Your journey back to wonder, joy, bliss, and full consciousness has begun. Embrace your new path forward with vigor, and step forward with confidence and assurance.

The other reason that the naming of space does not surprise you is that you already understand "space" in dimensional terms. You already have a strong experience of it. Everybody who is "in body" does. From the moment you open your eyes to the moment you breathe your last breath, you know with absolute certainty what space is all about. It is something you live in and experience every waking moment of your life. Space is also something easy to understand, and easy to specify, especially since you live it every day. While in body, we experience space as the distance between two points in creation. Put another way, we could say that while we inhabit a physical body, space is the difference between here and there. Saying it this way, we could then write out our definition of space like so.

Space

> Space = the difference between here and there

And that is really all there is to it. Space is simply the difference between here and there, the distance between two points in the physical universe. To this definition I just need to add that while in body we experience space as a *limitation*, specifically a limitation of location. That is, *while in body* you cannot be both here and there at the same time. You are where you are, and that is the end of it. Where your body is located is where your body is located, period.

However it is important to note at this point that the experience of this new dimension of space is different for Spirit. While in Spirit, when you are not "encumbered" with a physical body, you experience space (and time for that matter) entirely differently. While in Spirit we do not experience space as the difference between here and there because in Spirit *there is no here and there.* In Spirit there is only consciousness and consciousness is a mere dot. In fact, consciousness is less than a dot because a dot has physical existence and consciousness does not. Consciousness does not exist in space or time. In fact, it is the other way around. Consciousness is the root reality and space and time exist within consciousness. In this context, i.e. within consciousness, space has no "real" physical existence. It is just something that happens as "I" dream the dream of the Unfolding. In the body it feels like distance; in Spirit it is something else altogether.

So how does Spirit experience space?

Well, since space is contained within consciousness, you can understand how Spirit experiences space if you consider the contents of consciousness. At the most fundamental level, consciousness consists of ideas and nothing more. These ideas can be packaged or organized in certain ways in order to give us experiences, but at root, consciousness is merely a complex collection of ideas, and ideas are the sole content of consciousness. Thus, in this context, if Spirit has any experience of space at all, Spirit must experience space as something to do with ideas.[49] There is no other possibility.

With this understanding of consciousness in mind, and with the understanding that space is only an idea in consciousness, only a dream inside the mind of "I," the question before us becomes, if there is nothing but ideas in consciousness, how does Immortal Spirit experience space? Where does the notion of "here" and "there" fit into all this when the reality is that only ideas exist? Well, that is simple. As Immortal Spirit, we experience space as nothing more than the difference in interest between ideas. We can state this in formula form below.

----

[49] This is true for all dimensions/sephiroth. All features and factors of creation must be derivable from the basic nature of consciousness. And since consciousness is really nothing more than a collection of ideas (ideas about creation, ideas about self, etc.), all sephiroth must be rooted in ideas, the relationship between ideas, the interaction of ideas, and so on.

Space in Spirit

> Space (or distance) is the difference in interest
> between ideas manifested in energy

The phrase *difference in interest* is the key phrase here, so pay attention. It cannot be stated with any more clarity. When we do not have a body to encumber us, ideas and the things they represent are close to us when we are interested and paying attention, and far away from us when we are disinterested and preoccupied elsewhere.

Now, consider this.

In the beginning, when there was only "I." there was no space.

In the beginning, when there was only "I," there was no distance between ideas.

In the beginning, when there was only "I" and "I" was omniscient and omnipresent, "I" was interested in everything, and whatever "I" was interested in was all in mind *at the same point* and at the same time. As such, in the beginning, there was no space between ideas. Everything was all there "at the surface" for "I" to see, and intend, and manipulate. And thus was the condition of creation in the beginning. In the beginning there were no dimensions, no perspective, no chance, no time, and no space; just the inimitable, illimitable, "I" dancing an exquisite and eternal dance of "I-ness," with all ideas packed together into one tight little *idea ball* that never got any bigger or smaller but simply was.

Interestingly enough this little idea ball, this concentrated dream in the mind of "I," didn't change much for the first couple of levels in the Unfolding. In the beginning there was no space, and for the next five levels, there was no space. This is because even as "I" added "yous" to the Fabric of Consciousness, "we" did not generate enough ideas to press apart our individual interest in things. As individualized Sparks of the One, we are all quite powerful and capable of being aware of many things at once and so in the early stages, all things were contained within the single "space" of a non-dimensional "us." In the beginning all things were part of our awareness and thus there was no space between ideas.

This was true at the second and third levels of creation, however at the fourth and fifth level of the Unfolding, things started to change. At these levels there were enough monads in consciousness to create distance between ideas. Things were changing and ideas were moving apart. At the fourth and fifth level we were starting to develop our own specialties and as we did that, we often paid less attention to what was going on with someone else. Space existed, therefore, but at the fourth and fifth level too many other things were going on and we just didn't notice. However, at the sixth level, when we got to 137,370,551,967,459,378,662,586,974,208 monads (a big jump from five billion) the space between our ideas was no longer unimportant, insignificant, or unnoticeable. With that many monads, the number of ideas in creation expanded beyond the desire and capacity of any single monad (including the original "I" in creation) to be aware of at all times.

It came down to this.

With that many monads working on that many projects, "I" didn't necessarily care about what you were doing. "I" might be wrapped up in my blue crystal palace while you were wrapped up in your manifestation of an elegant garden and "I" just didn't want to expend the effort to pay attention to what you were doing. Not that your garden wasn't important or interesting, of course, but "I" had enough on my plate with my stuff and simply wasn't interested in what you were doing all the time.

Even "I" found that it was more fun to focus because "I" missed less that way.

And "I" wasn't the only one.

As consciousness continued to unfold, we all became interested in a different combination of creative ideas. We stopped following everything that was going on and started paying attention to only what interested us. No longer following what the other one was doing, we were individualizing and creating our own unique little boxes in creation. When that happened, the ideas we were not interested in faded from our monadic consciousness and "we," and "I," lost the omniscient omnipresent character of consciousness interfacing with creation.

God with a big "G", God with a little "g"

Now depending on your religious background, at this point you may feel a little uncomfortable. In fact for some I might be tweaking some deeply embedded fear at this point. God/Consciousness/Krishna or whatever you want to call it is supposed to be omniscient, omnipresent, and all-powerful.

Now here I am telling you that this is not the case. If this worries you or concerns you, do not be concerned because in fact even though at the sixth level of creation god loses the defining quality of omniscient, omnipresent, omnipotence, God does not. That is, even at the sixth level of creation, even with the instantiation of a ridiculously large number of new monads, even with the limitations on our attention and interest, God is still omniscient and omnipresent.

But wait!??

Didn't I just say that God was not omniscient and omnipresent? I admit it, I did, but that is because it is both. At the sixth level of the Unfolding, when the dimension of space pops into existence, there is both omniscience and omnipresence, and not. We can resolve this apparent contradiction by simply making a distinction between God with a big "G" and god with a little "g".

God with a big "G" is the Fabric of Consciousness *in toto*.

God with a big "G" is the Tree of Light from trunk to tip.

God with a big "G" is the conscious Water of Creation.

God with a big "G" is the entire ball of wax.

On the other hand, god with a little "g" is the individual, instantiated monad.

God with a little "g" is a light on the Tree of Light.

God with a little "g" is an "eye" in the Fabric of creation.

God with a little "g" is god the monad looking at creation, but not necessarily seeing all the details all at once.

God with a little "g" is "I," and "you",

God with a big "G" is "we," and "us".

Now, whether or not you can say that "god" is omniscient and omnipresent depends entirely on whether you are referring to God with a big "G", or god with a little "g". If you are referring to the former, then yes, God is omniscient and omnipresent, and space holds no meaning! That is because God with a big "G" is the entire Fabric of Consciousness and when you take the Fabric in toto then nothing is going on within the Fabric that is not known. On the other hand if you are referring to the latter, then no, god is not omniscient and omnipresent. God with a little "g" is an individual monad in a vast Fabric of consciousness. God with a little "g" is a little "I" in vast oceans of awareness. God with a little "g" is aware and powerful, but focused, and so not everything that is happening in the vast Fabric is available to god with a little "g." Thus for god with a little "g," space is a valid dimension. This is not a bad thing. In fact, it is a good thing. It is exactly what we want. It is a new dimension of creation, a new factor in the equation, and this brings deviation, variation, and creative interest. And that is always a good thing.

And thus was space and distance born.

And thus was space experienced.

The less interest any individual "I" has in aspects of creation, the farther away those aspects of creation are. The more interested an individual "I" is, the closer it is.

Now, as you might gather, at the sixth level, with so many new monads instantiated in the Fabric, distances can become quite vast. As creation unfolds and new levels are added it is even possible to forget aspects of creation altogether. We get so wrapped up in our own little localities that we retain only a vague idea of what's going on "over there." If we stay in "our own space" too long we may even lose complete touch with the work of others. Just as our work evolves, so does theirs and the longer we stay away, the more different their work will become. Developments that occur while we are not paying attention will become unknown to us. As this occurs, we can get pretty isolated from certain aspects of creation if things evolve without our attention too long. If we lose total touch with another aspect of creation, we may not even be able to see the light given off without a telescope. In this situation *the creations of others simply fade off into the distance and darkness of space.*

But again, this is not a bad thing.

It is true that we lose touch with certain ideas in creation in order to focus on our important ideas, but this is not a permanent sacrifice. This does not mean that we develop a limiting creative isolation. The connection between monads in the Tree of Consciousness is constant and inviolate and as such it is always easy[50] to draw near to any idea in creation, while in Spirit, if you so choose. You may even go so far as to change your entire *constellation* of interests when it is of interest to you. It is a question of choice only. We ultimately

---

[50] While in Spirit.

choose our more limited perspectives and concerns because we find it desirable to do so. If at any point we choose another perspective, another constellation, another galaxy, or even another universe of ideas, we may.

I suppose a question that may arise now is, why choose to focus rather than generalize? Isn't omniscient, omnipresent, omnipotence the only way to go?

Certainly not!

It comes down to a question of interest and personal craftsmanship.

An example will perhaps help to sort this out.

Imagine for a moment that you are a practicing pianist. As anyone who engages in any sort of manual skill development will know (and this would include playing an instrument, building a house, or nurturing a garden) it takes years of practice and dedication to reach the level of "master." From the manual skill of moving your fingers to the more ethereal ability to really play the instrument, it takes effort, patience, work, and focus. In fact, it takes so much will and so much effort that if you want to be a master carpenter, master gardener, or master pianist, you are going to have to choose among the things you do. The bottom line is, to get really good at something you will have to *give other things up* while you focus on your one thing. A concert pianists practices hours a day, and since there is only so much time in a day, only so much focus and attention may be given. Of course, this is not a problem for those who love playing the piano, or who love building, and so on. This is a choice they make in order to be able to attain the level of mastery they seek. They make this choice, and are happy doing it, because they love what they do.

It is a tradeoff, really.

We sacrifice one thing so we can become/experience more of another. A concert pianist gives up a daily walk in the park in order to develop skill and master her instrument. A master carpenter gives up learning to play an instrument in order to create beautiful structures.

It is a sacrifice, to be sure, but if you love something enough it is hardly a sacrifice at all.

It is quite like this in creation.

The more we create, the more ideas we have, and the more our repertoire of imaginings expands, the more it becomes desirable to focus on some things and ignore others. It is merely a question of craftsmanship and interest. The more you want to work with the details, the more you want to become a master of (particular types of) manifestation, the more you will need to create space between your interests and the interests of others. Just how much space we will put between us and the ideas of others, and how many ideas we will ignore in our quest for craftsmanship, will depend entirely on personal choice and creative purpose. Some monads do many things at once and others focus on single tasks to the point of ethereal mastery. Some assume wider perspectives, and others narrow down. The field is totally open and there is no limitation imposed by your particular place in the Unfolding. There is no sense in which you are confined to a box, required to do anything, be at any level, or undertake any task. You do what you want to do with the monads you want to do it with, within a space defined by you for purposes of pursuing your creative goals.

To summarize: You create space because you want to and need to, and you experience space as simply the distance between ideas in your consciousness.

Before moving on I have one little detail to clear up. I imagine a question that must be in your minds right now is, how do we bridge distances created by diverging ideas in consciousness? Or, in the language of the body, how do we get from "here" to "there" efficiently? As it turns out, while we are a free Spirit, i.e., while we are not "confined" in the body, it is easy. All we have to do to bridge a distance is take an interest in something. As soon as you start to take an interest in something, you start to draw that idea into your consciousness and the distances begin to collapse. How fast that idea gets into your consciousness will depend on things like how far the idea is away from your own conceptual patterns, how interested you are in it, how big the idea is, how much focus and attention you give, etc. The idea of a piano, for example, is smaller and has a smaller subset of ideas than the idea of a galaxy and so you can get close to pianos quickly. Moving to a new galaxy of ideas, on the other hand, can take a little extra effort, especially if the ideas used to construct the internal workings of said galaxy are different than the ideas used to construct your local experience. You may have a lot to learn before you can completely transcend the distance and absorb yourself in the new galaxy. However, not to worry, you will get there if you want. While in Spirit, there are no limitations.

Of course, it is not the same while in body. The limitations of space you experience while in body are not so easy to overcome. Unlike your consciousness, which can be anywhere and do anything at any time, your body is limited by its location in space. This is actually quite important, so go slowly here. The phrase, "Your body is limited by its location in space," really means your body is limited by its location in a constellation of ideas. Remember, your body is a part of creation. It is made up of the energies of creation organized by a particular subset of ideas. Your body is thus an idea of individuality, within an idea of life, within the idea of Earth, within an idea of Sol (i.e., the Sun), within the idea of the Milky Way, within the idea of this physical universe, etc. and its location in the constellation of ideas absolutely defines its location.

Pay close attention here, now.

As long as you take the perspective of the idea (i.e., the perspective of your body), your body is locked in its location. However, this limitation of "here" and "there" only arises because of the perspective you take. It is not a necessary feature of creation. That is, the fact that the idea that your body is confined to a certain location within physical creation does not mean that your body is necessarily confined to that location. It is not a matter of the physical laws of the physical universe that say that physical matter cannot be in more than two places at once, or that it cannot jump from location to location with impunity.[51] There are no "natural laws" in the universe like that. All physical laws of the physical universe are linked to ideas in consciousness and ideas can always be changed. Therefore the physical laws of the universe are mutable. This is beside the main point here, however. The main point isn't to discuss the technical mutability of the physical "laws," the point is to underline the possibility of overcoming the spatial limitations of your physical body.

So, how do you overcome the confinement of your physical body?

Well it is easy to understand but difficult (though not impossible) to implement. It has to do with the movement of ideas. Remember, your body is an idea within a set of ideas. Thus the location of your body is defined by the ideas that surround it. Therefore, all you have to do to change the location of your body is to change the surrounding ideas. This is easy to say, but hard to accomplish. The difficulty that we experience here arises because of the group nature of most of creation, and the fact that our group (i.e., the group on this earth) has existed beneath a Veil that has prevented our access to spiritual truths for a long, long time. The true power and glory of our creation has been kept from us, and the limited perspectives of a veiled existence have been normalized to the point where limitation is what we have come to know, and to expect. Thus even the simplest Truths of Spirit have been hidden from us and so most of us would

---

[51] In fact, I believe physicists are starting to realize that matter "jumps around" all the time.

173

not even consider the possibility of moving our bodies in space like that. It's made even harder by the fact that many of us become fearful at the mere thought of somebody else "imposing" an idea in our consciousness. Sadly, if even one of the group is not open to the idea emerging in their consciousness, you will not be able to portal into the room. But it is possible if we all realize it is. Creation is a collective process and we all (or at least a significant number of us) have to believe in high magic if high magic is going to work.[52] I'll discuss this more in advanced LP teachings, but for now you can start preparing by beginning the difficult process of shifting your "faith" from the material world to the spiritual realms. By starting to believe that this type of high magic is possible, you will be preparing your own bodily consciousness for the deeper shifts that will be required to realize these post-ascension siddhis.

Wrapping up the Unfolding

Now that we have completed our discussion of the dimension of space, we are pretty much at the end of Volume One of *The Book of Light*. We have covered a lot of ground even in this short tome and hopefully you will have gained significant

---

[52] This is one of the principle reasons why ascension is really a collective and not an individual process. All the promised magic of ascension will be easiest to accomplish and work best when most of us get the right ideas into our consciousness. Even Jesus needed a collectivity to believe before he could accomplish his task, which was to demonstrate the possibilities.

"enlightenment" as you have progressed through the work. You may have even had conscious shifts and connection experiences, especially if you approach this material in a receptive mode. You can test your progress forward, and the depth and breadth of your emerging enlightenment, by looking for several shifts in your metaphysical thinking processes. For example, you should now understand the true nature of consciousness. You should also understand the distinction between God and god. You should know the nature (i.e. creation is but a dream, literally) and purpose (to have fun and avoid boredom) of creation. You should also have some idea of the internal elements and processes of consciousness (summarized in ancient alchemical texts as the elements fire, air, water, and earth). You should understand your own relationship to all that is (i.e., you are all that is, but you are also an individual instantiated "eye" in the Fabric of Consciousness). You should understand the nature of dimensions and their relationship to consciousness and the Unfolding. Finally, you should understand the collective nature of creation and the importance of the *Collective Consciousness*, or *the Group*, to accomplishing manifestation tasks, especially larger ones.

This last one is particularly important and is a bit of a foundational idea. Creation is consciousness, and consciousness is ideas. Ideas in consciousness determine physical creation or, as I like to say, as above in consciousness, so below in matter. It is important to understand that at this point in the Unfolding, with so many instantiated monads paying attention to creation, creation is never an individual thing, but a collective thing. Although individual intent is important, and can be determinative, far more significant is our collective orientation to reality, and our collective intent. It is the condition and state of our collective consciousness, and the force and direction of our collective intent, that determines the state of creation. In this context we have to pay attention to the number of monads working on a thing. The bottom line is, the more monads focusing on a thing, the more likely that thing is to manifest. This is a basic, and key, principle of "high magic."

This principle of "high magic" is something you need to understand for a couple of reasons. On the one hand, this is an important principle because of its significance to individual creation. If you want to be effective at the individual level, you have to pay attention to the collective context! Put another way, individual intent is always important, but collective intent has a bigger impact. Recall our monad Sparkle. She can't get her dramatic red flash until she gets more monads on board. The collective consciousness of the Fabric creates a creative direction, and an experience of inertia, that an individual monad can only overcome by bringing more monads "on board." This important creative principle is, incidentally, alluded to in the Christian Bible, in the context of "drawing down" and manifesting the context of consciousness. Thus in Matthew 18 we hear Christ saying:

> Truly I say to you, whatever you shall bind on earth shall be bound in heaven: and whatever you shall loose on earth shall be loosed in heaven. Again I say to you, that if two of you shall agree on earth as touching anything that they shall ask, it shall be

done for them of my Father which is in heaven. For where two or three are gathered together in my name, there am I in the middle of them. **Matthew 18:20**[53]

You can properly contextualize the above quote by replacing the notion of "Father in heaven" with the notion of Fabric of Consciousness or God with a big "G". If you do that you'll see the Bible talking about high magic, and will understand the importance of the collective nature of creation.

Now, on the other hand the principle of the collective nature of creation is important because it points to the incredible significance of our collective consciousness. When two or more people share a set of ideas, these ideas tend to manifest and stick with greater force. This makes the contents of the collective consciousness incredibly important! Your little spot on the Canvas is your little spot on the Canvas, that is true, however your spot on the Canvas, the paint you use, the monads around you, and even the Canvas itself, are functions of the sum total of all ideas in the Fabric.[54] *If you want to understand* creation and manifestation, and why it is the way it is, then this means understanding the ideas in consciousness. More importantly, because of the *inertia* caused by collective

---

[53] I am sure if we looked hard enough we would see the idea represented in Matthew 18:20 reflected in many of the other classic spiritual works of this planet, like the Bhagavad Gita, for example.

[54] Or at least those ideas "close" to you.

intent in the Fabric, *if you want to change* manifestation in some way, say add a thing or two, or even change direction altogether, then *the place to work* is at the collective level of consciousness, with the collectively shared ideas (or archetypes as I like to say) that govern the quality, content and direction of manifestation in creation. There is no other way. Any sophisticated attempt at creation and manifestation, any attempt to *change direction,* or *paint a new picture,* will have to take into account the collective consciousness of an area, and will have to work at modifying the ideas and archetypes in that consciousness. As I like to say:

As above in consciousness, so below in matter

The contents of our collective consciousness are determinative of the reality we manifest.

This is incredibly important, and becomes highly significant later on in our studies[55] when we look at "system" archetypes in the collective consciousness of this planet, so I am going to ask you to repeat the statement until the idea of archetypes, the collective consciousness, and the collective nature of manifestations, is burned into your memory.

Repeat.

Any attempt to change direction must take into account the collective consciousness of an area.

Any attempt to paint a new picture will necessarily involve modifying the ideas and archetypes in the collective

---

[55] In particular the LP Intermediate Module B – Archetypal Study.

consciousness of the Group.

Repeat.

Any attempt to change direction must take into account the collective consciousness of an area. *Any attempt to paint a new picture* will necessarily involve modifying the ideas and archetypes in the collective consciousness of the Group. Please repeat until this is burned into your memory.

The Story of the Unfolding

As noted above, the significant revelations of this volume of The Book of Light have been accomplished. You know about dimensions, the collective nature of creation, the Unfolding, and so on. There is more to come in The Book of Light Volume Two, but before we go there we need to complete our story of the Unfolding. At this point we don't have a lot to say since most of the important stuff has already been said. All we really have to do is complete our account of the "first stage" of the Unfolding, and we can do that fairly quickly.

First of all, recall our accounting thus far. At the point we started discussing the high magic of creation we were at the sixth level of the unfolding. At this level the monadic pyramid that underlies creation looked like this:

1

2

12

1,728

5,159,780,352

137,370,551,967,459,378,662,586,974,208

Also remember that at this sixth level we had attained five new dimensions in creation. We had attained detail, perspective, chance, time, and space. The relationship between the levels and the dimensions is outlined in the figure below.

Levels and Dimensions/Sepiroth of Creation

1st Level = O Dimension = no dimensions
2nd Level = 1st Dimension = perspective
3rd Level = 2nd Dimension = detail
4th Level = 3rd Dimension = chance
5th Level = 4th Dimension = time
6th Level = 5th Dimension = space

When the Unfolding is represented like this, we can easily see the layered (though not hierarchical) nature of consciousness, the quantitative and qualitative features of emanation/Unfolding, and the linear realization of dimensions/sephorith. At this point it is perfectly reasonable to expect the rest of the story to follow the same layered and linear process, and that is in fact what happens (at least at this first stage of creation). Thus, in order to complete our overview of the Unfolding all we have to do is complete the layers and list the additional dimensions that come into play. The only question we need to answer to accomplish that is how far does the Unfolding ultimately go? That is, does the Unfolding go on for infinity or is there some point where we stop? If we do stop, where do we stop? At what level do we call a halt to the proceedings?

Well, the truth is, we do not go on for infinity. As we shall see, we cannot keep adding new layers and new monads. A point does come when there are simply too many monads to continue any further. That point happens at the 13th level of consciousness. At that point (at the point where you are currently peeking out into creation), we call a halt to the process and leave ourselves with a final pyramid of consciousness that looks like this.

1

2

12

1,728

5,159,780,352

137,370,551,967,459,378,662,586,974,208

2.5922741544123682944025175270975e+87

1.7419784962119569043779248369980e+262

5.2860147265533822475587345746700e+786

1.4770156811849031906483197809621e+2360

3.2222096096844682399043129705670e+7080

3.3455379095640236110097154751979e+21241

3.7445347579428565357376535631063e+63724

I agree, it is a mind-boggling number of monads, and that, dear one, is the problem. At the 13th level of the Unfolding, there are simply too many monads in creation, and we cannot go any further with the Unfolding without running into significant technical obstacles.

Now don't misunderstand.

We can continue to add monads forever if we want to.

There is no limit to the number of monads we may add.

The problem isn't a technical one, the problem here is a practical one.

The problem arises because of the unrestrained expansion of the dimensions.

Remember, the amount of any dimension increases in a predictable way with the number of monads in creation. This has been part of our discussion since the beginning. Whenever I introduced a new dimension into your awareness, I always made it a point to underline the fact that the amount of any dimension (i.e., its quantity) is dependent on the number of monads working in creation. You will recall the formulaic representation of this with regards to chance.

$$T_{otal}Chance = fnMonads$$

We could write a formula like this for any of the dimensions (i.e., space, time, perspective, detail, and chance) but we won't do that. The point here is simply that the amount of any single dimension is always a function of the number of monads. Put as simply as possible, the more monads there are in the Fabric, the more of a particular dimension there will be.

And that is the nub of the problem!

Because the quantity of a dimension expands as the number of monads increases, because the total amount of any given dimension is a function of the number of monads working in the Fabric, a point comes when creation becomes difficult and precarious because there is simply too much of a certain dimension, in this case inertia and time.[56] I realize this is all a little abstract so in order to ground our understanding and get an intuitive sense of this problem, let us frame the issue by asking the following questions:

- What happens when there is too much chance in creation?

- What happens when there is too much inertia (or time)?

The answers to the above questions are easy.

- If there is too much time (or inertia), creation takes too long and requires too much effort.

- If there is too much chance, creation comes apart too easily (i.e., there are too many chance things happening) and too much concentration is required to keep things on track.

Consider the dimension of chance as an example.

You already understand that the more monads there are, the more chance there will be in creation. You also know that the more chance there is, the more random events (i.e., events

---

[56] As a side note here, you should be aware that not all dimensions are implicated in our difficulty. That is, not all dimensions reach the point where there is too much. The actual problem is limited to only a couple of dimensions, namely inertia (i.e., time), and chance. Perspective, detail, and space never become problematic.

caused by the unintentional crossover of intent) will occur. There is nothing magical here. With so many monads in creation, things tend to get a little crowded and uncertain. This is not a fundamentally bad thing, it is simply a thing. It is simply that too many painters painting on the same canvas creates a bit of chaos. With too many painters there will be a lot of stray paint splashes, a lot of color bleed, etc. With a lot of painters in the room there will be a high level of creative "noise" and this noise will become more and more of a problem the more monads come on line. When things get crowded enough, it will become impossible for any single monad to get what they want. There will be too much interference from the crowd, and too much noise in the room, and consequently manifesting desire will become difficult, if not totally impossible. The bottom line is, in the Unfolding of consciousness there will come a point when there is too much chance and we will "lose control" over the energy of creation.

Please understand this isn't the type of loss of control that leads to a downward spiral into chaos. As we have already discussed, that is not possible. Energy never gets out of control in that sense and if it did, we'd all just unplug from the matrix and that would be the end of it. What I'm talking about here when I say loss of control is simply the inability to focus ideas into energy and get the intended results. For example, I paint a blue square and somebody else splashes green and pink (yuck, I know) on my blue square, and now I have a brown, smudgy mess. I exert intent for squareness, but somebody else draws a line and now I have two triangles.

It can get extremely frustrating. In fact, under conditions like this (i.e. too much chance), manifestation becomes downright annoying. Creation becomes too much of an effort and no fun at all. Intent keeps crossing over and things keep happening to our creation and we spend so much *intention* and *attention* trying to control things, that moving forward with our ideas becomes no fun at all. And when that happens, when creation becomes "no fun at all," then we have lost the entire point of creation.

The same sort of problem arises with the dimension of time/inertia as well. After a certain point in creation, there is simply too much inertia and getting anything done requires too much time. Just think back to Sparkle for this one. It is one thing to convince a hundred monads of the usefulness of intending red in a palace of blue, but try doing the same with five million, or five trillion. It is true we are all connected, but this doesn't mean we are all close to each other. Getting "the message" out to that many monads can be extremely difficult and *time consuming* and while it is always possible to limit the number of monads in a group (and in fact this is something that is practiced all the time, see our discussion of the multiverse below), ultimately we are all part of one BIG group, and when that group gets too big, inertia becomes too strong and manifesting takes too long. It is at this point, when there is too much chance and too much inertia, and when creation gets to be too tedious, that we call a halt to the Unfolding. At this point creation is requiring too much time and effort, and we simply do not want to go forward. In fact, we really cannot move forward. If we did, if we moved forward to the fourteenth level of the Unfolding by applying the Tradition again and cubing the bottom layer to get another level, there would be so many monads generating so much chance and so much time that creation would grind to a jittering halt.

So what did we do then when we got to the end of the thirteenth level and realized we could no longer add more monads? There were two things we could do. One, we could go back to the start. If we couldn't find a way forward we could simply unwind the Unfolding, melt all the instantiated monads back into a unified Fabric, return to "oneness," (i.e. when only "I" existed), and start over. At this point though, that was not an option. Nobody in the Fabric wanted to return to oneness. Not only would that be no fun, but so much experience, so many memories, and so much knowledge and wisdom would simply fold into oblivion. In short, we would all *lose our identity,* and nobody wanted that. Thus, the only way forward was to find something new to do. Of course, finding something new to do was going to be a bit of a problem. Having reached the practical limits of the Unfolding, we simply did not know what we would do next. We had been "unfolding" for so long that we were kind of stumped at first. But that didn't last long. As you already know, we have eternity to ponder and in the Unfolding of eternity, no problem can ever go unsolved. Thus we eventually found a solution.

There were a couple of things we did. On the one hand, and in order to change things up a bit, we "jumped in" to the Water of Creation in order to play "from the inside out." I'll explain more about this in volume two of this Book of Light. On the other hand we also decided we needed to change the rules. We decided to alter the dimensional mix and ascend the universe in an effort to beat the Problem (i.e. the problem of ennui and boredom) and continue on with our playtime. I summarize the Ascension in The Book of Life: *Ascension and the Divine World Order*, and also talk about that in subsequent volumes of this Book of Light (in particular volume four). Before we can get into all that however there are a couple of loose ends that need to be tied up.

The Multidimensional Multiverse and the Watershed of Creation

The Multiverse

The first loose end comes from a misconception that I have allowed to percolate into this document. I know that up until this point I have given the strong impression that the problem of chance and time only become critical factors at the thirteenth level of the Unfolding, but that's not true. The truth is, time and chance begin to be problems much earlier on in the Unfolding. Indeed, we actually start running into difficulty in intention and attention at the ninth or tenth level of the Unfolding. The thing is, however, *we do not run into a wall* at the ninth or tenth level like we do at the thirteenth. We have problems with time and chance, but at those early levels we were are able to find stopgap solutions, solutions that staved off the inevitable wall, and gave us more time to play. What we basically did to solve the problem of expanding time and chance was *partition* creation into compartments. We created little boxes where huge numbers of monads (which we might call Super Groups [57]) could break off to work on separate creative tasks.

This partitioning had a couple of benefits. On the one hand it helped reduce the practical impact of the problematic dimensions of time and chance. In the boxes, the super groups are isolated from each other as far as is possible. In our individual Super Groups we all stay interested in our own "little" boxes, and we put up "do not enter" signs in order to request non-interference. Monads in the other boxes stay away and stay involved in their own work, and in this way we build little galaxies and big *alternate universes* where Super Groups can work with reasonable numbers of monads, and reasonable amounts of time and chance. This was (and is) an excellent way to stave off the inevitable end of the Unfolding. Reducing the total amount of monads paying attention to any given universe allowed each Super Group to keep control over the problem dimensions. It allowed them to reduce the total amount of chance and time to manageable levels–at least temporarily.

Another benefit of creating partitions in creation was that the partitioning allowed us to experiment with rule sets. Different boxes, different partitions, different *universes,* could have different creative characteristics. One universe could be "like this", and the other universe could be "like that". That is, one universe could have one set of physical constants, and a certain array of forces keeping all things together, and the

---

[57] Or galaxies.

other universe could have a totally different set of rules, constants, and forces.

This was a great thing!

Having alternative universes allowed us to experiment in ways previously unimagined. We were able to create entire universes vastly different from our own, but equally wondrous, glorious, and powerful. Not only was this incredibly interesting for us, but it also added amazing levels of deviation and variation. Couple the deviation and interest of multiple universes with the fact that we were able to stave off the inevitable dimensional crunch of the Unfolding and we were able to extend our forward movement up until the thirteenth level. Of course, it couldn't last forever. At some point we would explore the full potential of even a multidimensional universe, and something would need to be done. That point came at the thirteenth level. At the thirteenth level we had explored the deviation and variation of multiple universes to the point of ennui. Thus further partitioning made no sense at all. It might reduce inertia and time, but it would be more of the same on all fronts. And so it was that at the thirteenth level of creation our multidimensional, multi-layered, omni-verse of creation came to a shuddering, grinding, halt, not because chance and inertia suddenly became a problem (they had been a problem for a while), but because the partitioning that could help us localize creation and reduce inertia and chance was no longer an option. At that point something new had to be found to move us all forward. As noted above, those two things were the *Watershed,* and the *Ascension.* The ascension we will explore in more detail in volume four, the Watershed we will introduce next, and develop further in volume two.

The Watershed

Before closing off this volume and moving on to volume two, there is one final loose end to clear up. The first loose end was the need to get you over the idea that it was only at the sixth level of the Unfolding that time and chance occurred. I did that and in the process introduced the idea of the multiverse into our discussion of the Unfolding. The second loose end is the need to clarify the dimensional nature of the Fabric. Recall at this point the earlier illustration of the dimension and levels of creation.

Dimensions and Levels of Creation

1st Level = O Dimension = no dimensions
2nd Level = 1st Dimension = perspective
3rd Level = 2nd Dimension = detail
4th Level = 3rd Dimension = chance
5th Level = 4th Dimension = time
6th Level = 5th Dimension = space

I introduced this overview at the sixth level of the Unfolding, and then went on to summarize the Unfolding to the thirteenth level. In this summary there was only a discussion of the problem of chance and inertia, and only a presentation of the little boxes of creation as a solution. I did not talk about any new dimensions at any of the levels in between. However, given the previous levels of the Unfolding and the fact that a new dimension (or factor) had popped at each new level, it would be reasonable to expect that at the seventh level of the Unfolding, some new dimension would emerge.

1st level =no dimensions

2nd level = 1st Dimension = perspective

3rd level = 2nd Dimension =detail

4th level = 3rd Dimension =chance

5th level = Dimension = time

6th level = 5th Dimension = space

7th level = 6th Dimension = ????

Looking at it now, it seems sensible and natural to expect a new dimension at the seventh level. And in fact, we, the monads in creation, did expect it. Because we had been through it a few times before we, as immortal Spirit, expected to continue to see emergent dimensions as long as we continued with the Unfolding; one new level leading to one new dimension, and on into eternity. Thus the only questions we had at the seventh level were, what was the new dimension going to be? Unfortunately, it did not work out that way. At the seventh level of creation we ran into an unforeseen block. At the seventh level we instantiated new monads, *but no emergent dimension was realized!*

At first it was slightly amusing, and fun, searching for the new factor. It was like a cosmic game of hide and seek. We laughed and danced while we played our first game of peek-a-boo in creation, looking for some new factor to emerge as monads were added exponentially. Unfortunately, no matter how much we looked, and no matter how much we danced, the new dimension did not emerge. It was odd, we had to admit. At all previous levels something had emerged. We had perspective, detail, chance, time, and space, one after the other in perfect spiritual form. Sadly though it did not happen at the seventh level and nothing we did made a shred of difference. At a certain point we finally had to accept the fact that there was going to be no new dimension. It was a major disappointment. Each previous level of the Unfolding had brought with it a new factor, a new dimension of creation to play with. Each new dimension created deviation, variation, and interest. But now, no new thing emerged, and it seemed that no new thing was going to emerge. After searching high and low, finally we accepted the fact that we, the monads of creation, had arrived at our first dimensionless level in the Unfolding, a dimensionless dimension (or dimensionless sephiroth) that we'll call daath.

Daath

At this point the cabalists among you should be picking your jaws up off the floor. The one place on this veiled earth where some sense of the "dimensionless dimension" of The Unfolding was preserved is in the cabalistic teaching of the Tree of Life. In that particular body of esoterica, a special sephira named Daath is set up and set apart from the others as a sort of black hole in creation. It is not always clear to the cabalists what Daath is all about, but it is always amazingly present in the teachings.

You can see this for yourself by

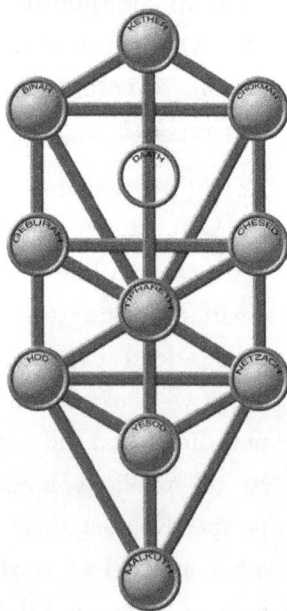

considering their illustration of the Tree of Life. Notice the empty, but not empty space near the top? That is Daath, the dimensionless sepiroth in creation. As you will now understand, Daath emerges at the point in the Unfolding where the quantitative addition of monads no longer leads to the qualitative emergence of a dimension/sephiroth.

Now, you may, if you wish, scrunch up your eyebrows, ponder and meditate with great severity on the sephira Daath. It has always been a tough esoteric nut to crack, and understanding what it is all about is a wonderful marker of your own progress. But do not get too hung up on this dimensionless dimension of the Unfolding. Despite the fact that it has drawn the attention of esoteric pundits from around the world, in the grander scheme, it is not that big a deal. Despite the fact that we lack an emergent dimension/sephiroth at the 7th level, this and subsequent levels are not that different from any of the other levels of the Unfolding. Beyond the significance of Daath as a motivator for the Watershed at the thirteenth level (see below), it is business as usual in that dimension. At the seventh level, creation still has monads, it still has all the previous dimensions (only in greater quantity), and it still has a wealth of opportunities for creative exploration. It is still a level in the Unfolding. It is just that it's a level without an emergent dimension popping into our awareness.

Really, it was no big deal. From a technical perspective the fact that we did not see a new dimension emerging in Daath was not a concern. From a technical perspective, it did not matter. We would still go about the business of play and exploration as usual. However, practically, I have to admit,

Daath was disappointing to all of us. By the seventh level of The Unfolding we had come to expect new and emerging dimensions. The search and surprise at discovery, and the new conditions brought about by the emergence of each new dimension, added a significant amount of enjoyment to our creative exploration, and it was sad to think that we would be unable to retrieve that fun.

It is also hard to overestimate the determination that grew out of our disappointment. We are Immortal Spirit after all. We are all the power in creation and we were not going to let a little technical burp like Daath stop us from having fun.

We knew what we had to do.

We had to take matters into our own hands.

We had to come up with something new.

Before we went any further in The Unfolding, we would have to ensure a new factor would emerge in creation that would be as exciting and titillating as the previous new dimensions had been.

But what?

And how?

It was a bit of a quandary, and I must admit we spent a considerable amount of consciousness on it. But of course, we did find a solution. In the unfolding of eternity, no problem ever goes without solution. And let me tell you, the solution we came up with was amazing.

It was wonder, bliss, joy.

It was breathtaking, it was orgasmic, it was a revolution in experience.

It was a watershed[58] in every sense of the word, and we will discuss this watershed and all its glorious implications, in Volume Two of The Book of Light.

---

[58] Merriam-Webster's Online Dictionary defines *watershed* as a crucial dividing point, line, or turning-point.

Conclusion

In this book we have examined the story of creation from "the beginning" through to a point just prior to the *Watershed* of creation. This Watershed occurs at the end of the 13th level of the Unfolding when there was too much time and too much chance to move forward, and when adding monads to the Fabric no longer triggered the emergence of new dimensions in the Fabric. In the process of telling the story of creation we have discussed the nature of god and God, *the Unfolding of Consciousness,* the multi-dimensional nature of creation as it emerges from consciousness, the emergence of the dimensions of creation (space, time), and so on. It has been, in my opinion and hopefully in yours, quite the journey. I hope this has been an enlightening journey for you. I hope The Book of Light has brought you depth of perspective and understanding that you did not have before. I hope you are more "enlightened" now than you were at the start. I hope you are becoming joyfully aware of your true nature. I hope you understand the creative process better. I hope you are becoming more confident and present in your daily life. Most importantly I hope The Book of Light has accomplished its primary goal, which is to shed light on the formally veiled and obscured (i.e. dark) corridors of cosmology and theology. In line with this, I hope by this point in the book whatever your spiritual background is you now understand the teachings of that background with greater depth, breadth, and insight than ever before. If this is the case for you then I have done my job and we can comfortably move on into deeper discussions of consciousness, God, and creation. Now that you know about the Fabric of Consciousness, now that you know about the Unfolding of Creation, now that you know about the instantiation of "I," "eye" and "will," now that you know about time, space, detail, and perspective, now it is time to look at the full depth and breadth of creation. Now it is time to look at the Watershed of Creation.

The next stage of this cosmological revelation will be quite interesting, I think. It will be interesting not only for the cosmological, theological and physical revelation it brings, but also because this point, i.e. the Watershed of Creation, is the point where we start talking about the universe that we created and that we live in, the universe you see around you. It is at this point that we start to take a look at the universe that we see with our own eyes, the one that we see when we gaze up at the stars at night. It might be a bit of a surprise to realize, but up until now our account of the Unfolding has come nowhere near an account of physical creation. As you will see clearly in the next volume, the creation of the universe that you see around you begins not "in the beginning" as discussed in this book, but somewhere in the middle. Indeed the truth is, this universe that enfolds you, this universe within which you move and manifest, is not even the first universe to exist, nor is it the last one. The truth is, creation bubbled into existence long, long, long before the bang that built this cosmos happened. Science only looks at what it can "see," and since it can't "see" behind the boundaries of this physical universe, it doesn't look any farther. The same holds true for biblical and some dogmatic accounts of creation. When the Bible says "God said, 'Let there be light,'" the accounting starts not in the real beginning, when only "I" existed, but at the Watershed of creation, when countless monads had already danced an eternal dance of creation. Creation, you see, is much bigger than we currently allow ourselves to think, after all. It is true. Christian or Buddhist, Hindu or scientists, our understanding of the depth of creation is limited and narrowly focused only on what we can "see" with our own eyes (i.e. the light in the sky).[59] The truth is, this universe is much bigger than even the most advanced "old energy" cosmologies have ever revealed. The truth is, the universe we live in is only a blink in the mind of God. The truth is, beyond the bang in consciousness that instantiated this universe is a creation so vast and so grand that there are simply no adjectives to describe it.

But, I'm jumping ahead. My point here is that starting in volume two of this *Book of Light*, we go deep and get a true sense of the depth and breadth of creation. Starting from the Watershed, we will look at this physical universe, how it came into existence, the physical mechanisms and laws which hold it together, and the relationship of all these to the Fabric (i.e. the consciousness) that underlincs it all. We will also look beyond the Watershed and put it into the context of the entire Unfolding. Starting in volume two, you will begin to see clearly the entire history of creation not from "the beginning"

---

[59] This is not true of the Sepher Yetzirah, and perhaps some Eastern account of creation. The SY, for all its clumsy and confused quality, starts in the *real beginning* and reveals creation as emanation from original "I" (or *ein soph* as I believe the kabbalists say).

of this universe, but from the beginning of all of creation. You will also see the location of this universe in creation (i.e. somewhere in the middle), and, by volume four, you will understand with clarity and precision why *this Earth* is so important.

This whole process should be a revelatory one for you (and me). Starting in the next volume and, and as we progress through the second, third, and fourth volumes of this series, your thinking about creation, and your understanding of your place in it, will rapidly expand and finally shatter the chains that have kept you sleeping and unaware of your true power and glory. This shattering of the chains may be instantaneous and powerful, occurring over the course of a few powerful and transformative visionary experiences, or it may be subtle and gentle, occurring in dreams, insight, and slow realization. However it occurs, it will occur. At this point in our current unfolding, it is necessary, and inevitable, and you cannot escape it. This planet is waking up no matter what, and there is nothing anybody can do to stop it now. The truth is there is no more space in this universe for blindfolded existence. The only question now is, how comfortable will you be as the revelation proceeds? Will you openly embrace expanded consciousness and awareness, and a deeper understanding of the cosmos and your place in it; or will fear, guilt, and confusion block the process and create internal struggle and conflict? It is an important question. We (and by "we") I mean the people of this Earth, have been trying for a long time to take off the blindfold and shrug off the Veil. To this day, and despite all our technological wizardry, we have not been all that successful in unwrapping the deep spiritual truths of creation. Science continues to be dominated by naïve materialism, and spiritual explanations have not (in my opinion) advanced much past the confused ramblings of blindfolded priests, profits, and pundits. Given our spiritual knowledge is still rather primitive, and given we have been trying for thousands of years to understand, obviously there is more to it than eating a mushroom or two, praying to Jesus to be your savior, meditating in silence, struggling with Enochian keys, or rubbing a singing bowl. If these approaches worked with as much efficiency and force as people claim, the world would have transformed centuries ago. The Truth is those approaches may (and often do) lead to brief glimpses of truth, to a slight rending of the Veil, but more often than not the glimpses are submerged by the facades of our daily life. They provide "teasers" of the Truth, and nothing more. If you want to take those teasers and build them into something permanent, you have to build the foundation, prepare the vessel for the light (for God, for consciousness, for the birth of the Christ within you, attainment of nirvana, etc.), and do the work.

I suppose the question (or questions as the case may be) now is, how do you openly embrace the light? How do you prepare the vessel for the light? How do you move forward with an expanding and joyful awareness? How do you avoid the fear, guilt, conflict, confusion, anger, and hatred that has halted so many others? These issues and questions are well beyond the scope of this work, but they are within the scope of the Lightning Path in general. For some preliminary guidance on preparing and opening to consciousness, see my *Great Awakening: Concepts and Techniques for Successful Spiritual Practice.*

That book provides an overview of key spiritual concepts and technique, gives you awakening advice and guidance, and provides a preliminary orientation to keep you safe and in control. When you are ready to move beyond the basic spirituality of the Great Awakening (which really only sets the foundation), more in-depth study and guidance can be found in Lightning Path study modules. These modules take a deep and expansive look at what you need to do to create conditions conducive to awakening and activation. Since Lightning Path modules are organized into levels of study, each of which builds upon the previous, you will want to start at the beginning, with the Lightning Path Core level. You can get an overview of available Lightning Path modules by visiting the link in the footnote[60] or the short description at the end of this book.

And that's all I have for you in this volume. In closing, let me just say that moving on beyond this point is very much an intentional process, a choice you make, and a discipline in which you engage. That is, you will not make any further progress forward until you make a choice, and do the work. I imagine many people reading this want to make the choice to move forward, and that's fine. The path has been set out and all you have to do is walk it. Keep in mind, though, that even though you are ready and willing at this point, even though you "make the choice" here, it is not a single choice you make. We live in a world that damages us, oppresses us, spins us

---

[60] See   http://www.thelightningpath.com/shop/lp-study-packages/ for available study packages.

around and distracts us. Thus an initial decision to expand consciousness and embrace your true inner light, and initial decision to walk the Path, is easily thwarted by the swirling toxicity of this planet. You may make the decision to move forward, and you may have all the discipline and intent to keep moving forward, but you may find yourself knocked off the path, pulled off the path, or even distracted by pretty lotus flowers growing on the side of the road.

It is the nature of the beast on this planet.

To avoid the unfortunate circumstance of getting pulled, pushed, or distracted, keep your will focused and your intent pure. I provide some guidance on keeping your intent pure in the *Great Awakening: Concepts and Techniques for Successful Spiritual Practice*. The advice there is important, and helpful, however now that you have read volume one of this *Book of Light* you can go beyond the little yellow sticky notes and begin a more intentional, directive, and meaningful process. To facilitate this process I have included, on the next page, a "prayer" for you to say every day, preferably in the morning as soon as you get up, and in the evening before you go to bed. This prayer is a sophisticated reminder and affirmation of identity. It is a summary of the revelation not only in this book, but in all volumes to come. *The Prayer* is designed to provide you with a daily *reminder* of who you are, where you came from, and what your true potential is. As it is probably still early in your awakening process, you may find this prayer useful in reminding yourself of the divine Truth of you. Please feel free to print this prayer out and practice it until you are comfortable that you can maintain continued conscious awareness of your true nature and divinity.

Maintaining a clear and consistent idea of your own divinity will help you to move your awakening and activation process forward faster.

Appendix One - The Prayer

I AM ALL THAT I AM.

I AM the Alpha
I AM the Omega.
I AM the Beginning without end.
I AM the Point (of all Awareness).
I AM the Bliss (of pure consciousness).
I AM the Seed (of the Unfolding).

I AM the Fabric and the Foundation.

I AM the AIR (of Inspiration)
I AM the WATER (of Manifestation).
I AM the FIRE (of Creation)
I AM the EARTH (in Manifestation).

I AM the Source.
I AM the Mirror.
I AM the Layers (of the Unfolding).
I AM the Dimensions (of Creation).
I AM the Light (in the Heavens).
I AM the Life (on this Earth).
I AM Limitless (in my Potential).

I AM God (with a capital G).

I AM ALL THAT I AM.

Appendix Two –
Mysticism Exposed

Greetings and welcome. The book that you have in your hand, this *Book of Light* (BOL), is the first of a four volume series that provides a complete revelatory cosmology and theology. This book, and the books that follow, are a statement of the nature of consciousness, the nature of physical creation, and the relationship between the two. Put another way, this is a complete revelation of the physical nature of creation and the consciousness that underlies it all. By the end of this four volume series you will have a complete theoretical (and possibly experiential) understanding of consciousness and physical creation. What's more, you will be able to link the mystical wisdom you gain from these books to other religious traditions with which you are familiar, including science. By the end of this series you will, in short, have answers to all of the key big questions.[61]

As noted above, this book is organized into four volumes. The entire series is entitled *The Book of Light: The Nature of God, the Structure of Consciousness, and the Universe Within You.* Volume one of the series is subtitled *Air,* volume two is subtitled *Water,* volume three is subtitled *Fire,* and volume four is subtitled *Earth.* This "alchemical sequence" was developed independently as a result of the mystical experiences and

---

[61] See http://www.thespiritwiki.com/index.php/Big_Questions

exploration by me, the author, but is in line with the order of creation as outlined in the *Sepher Yetzirah* (Kalisch, 2006 (1877)) and other mystical texts. It should be noted that the sequence of creation is neither mystified, misrepresented, obscured, or confused. Every effort was made to present pure, transparent, and clean mystical knowledge. What's more, the explanation of creative *emanation* from source that is provided here, and the mystical revelations provided in my other books, are grounded, or in the process of being grounded, in the psychological, sociological, and scientific theory of modern natural science. This is not meant as a negative judgment on past attempts. The human physical unit is confined by the concepts, ideas, culture, and environment in which it finds itself. Two thousand years ago the type of revelation provided here would have been impossible simply because the environment, culture, and state of general knowledge did not support it. In short, in the past, words and ideas were not available to adequately ground and express the high level truths of the mystic's exploration. Now, it is a different story. Advances in psychology, sociology, physics, chemistry, and so on create a foundation where mystical revelation can finally be satisfactorily grounded in physical reality. Put another way, the benefit of writing a "book of creation" from our modern vantage point is that we can understand better the physical parameters of creation and can reflect upon the connection between mystical revelation and the physical truths of physical creation in a way not possible even a hundred years ago. It is time, high time in fact, to write a new book of creation grounded in modern psychology and modern physical science. There is a potential here to end ten thousand years of mystical, philosophical, and scientific conflict and confusion.

This is not an unreasonable statement, though it may appear to be at first. As I note in Volume Two of this series there is a "common core" of mystical experience that all researchers can agree to. That is, anyone who has a mystical experience describes the characters and features of the experience in the same way. One aspect of the "common core" is *ineffability*, or the feeling of being "trapped by the inadequacy of what language can express" (Chen, Qi, Hood, & Watson, 2011, p. 662). People who have mystical experiences uniformly report that they struggle to adequately express the noetic and enlightening nature of their experience. They come to *know*, but they cannot speak. This is evident not only in the self-reports of mystics who have experiences, but also in the key writings themselves. An enlightened read of *Sepher Yetzirah*, or many other standard go-to mystical texts, seems to indicate that Abraham struggled mightily to express the revealed/noetic truths. But is this because there are now and forever more no words to describe his noesis? Or is it because there were simply no words at the time? As a mystic who has worked hard to ground and express my mystical and visionary experiences, I would argue that the mystic's problem is not the essential ineffability, mysterious, or esoteric nature of the mystical experiences, but the lack of adequate concepts and ideas.[62] There has been, up until

----

[62] There are other problems as well. Mystical experiences tend to be informationally dense. That is, a single vision or revelation may

recently, a missing framework, an absent zeitgeist, that made expression of high level truths impossible. Abraham could have struggled his entire life to adequately represent the knowledge revealed and written down in Sepher Yetzirah, but he would have ultimately, and necessarily, failed because the scientific frame and general empirical sophistication of our modern times would not be available for thousands of years.[63] The point of the matter here is that *ineffability* is not a necessary feature of mystical experience, or the result of an unbridgeable divide between scientific reality and mystical awareness, but is the result of a lack of scientific understanding. It is not that the words, concepts, and ideas needed to express high level mystical truths cannot exist, it is

---

contain, for example, an entire cosmological revelation, a complete *noesis* as it were. This is certainly true of the revelations in the Book of Light. Many of the details and perspectives in this book were revealed in informationally dense packages, and it takes time and effort to unwrap these packages. And we are not talking a few days, weeks, or even months. The first edition of this book was published in 2006 and I have been working on grounding and expressing the revelations since then. And the work still goes on. I know the general direction and content of all four volumes, but I am still working on properly expressing them. This requires not only a society capable of supporting scholarly labor of this nature and duration, but also a certain level of personal discipline, and a certain type of courage and commitment. If these are absent it becomes a problem for the mystic trying to ground their revelation.

[63] Not to mention he probably did not have the time or the support to engage in the required scholarly work.

that they did not exist until fairly recently.[64]

I think concepts and language became adequate to express high level mystical truths with the emergence of quantum mechanics and high energy physics early in the 20th century. Of course, the question at this point becomes why hasn't an adequate expression of mystical experience in the context of acceptable scientific conceptualizations been made if the language has been around for a while? There are two reasons

---

[64] Lack of existence of language may go a long way towards explaining the existence of the oceans of esoteric drivel that haunt the spiritual landscape of this planet. As A.E. Waite notes on page 68 of his introduction to the Sepher Yetzirah"...when we heard of Hermetic Orders, Brotherhoods of Luxor and the Veil of Isis, it was apt to be a cloak for every kind of false pretense, not to speak of imbecility of thought." (Kalisch, 2006 (1877)) In better words, spiritual truths are hidden behind esoteric barriers and linguistic verbiage not to protect the profane but to protect the people who do not understand, and who haven't a clue. It is hard to tell the difference between the wheat and the chaff when the chaff is surrounded by bucketfuls of esoteric verbiage. This is certainly true of Sepher Yetzirah which, in the hands of Western esotericists, became grounded in tortuous systems of esoteric correspondence that linked the twenty-two Hebrew letters to everything from the Tarot to psychology. The tortuous correspondences provide a protective covering that allows the confused brother to a) defend their ignorance as wisdom, b) accuse those who come with questions as lacking in preparation or understanding, or c) cover over their venal use of spiritual truths for economic and political gain (Sosteric, 2013b). Interestingly, the protective covering functions only so long as the words are not available. When the words become available, the meaning of the mystical experiences come into focus, the "veil" is dissipated, and the ridiculous and pompous nature of much esoteric "work" becomes painfully obvious even (perhaps especially) to the uninitiated.

for this I think. **One** is the general assumption that science and mysticism, or science and religion, are at opposite and antagonistic ends of an ontological and epistemological spectrum. The two areas are different, and unbridgeable, or so we believe, assume, and expect. I don't feel this is the case at all. I think the two realms have only appeared unbridgeable because attempts to bridge the spectrum have been abortive. This is because there is no adequate framework, no agreed upon linguistic core, that is suitable for both sides. To be as plain as possible, mystics talk mystical language and scientists talk scientific language and no effort is made to bring the two together. As a result, people either try to impose the language of science onto the experience of mysticism, or people try to impose the (often dated and inadequate) language of mystical experience onto science. Both approaches are ultimately abortive in my opinion. One leads to fluffy new age style expositions, the other leads to biased, arrogant, and mystically vacuous intellectual puffery. What is needed is to start in the middle, developing new concepts and ideas that work for both science and mysticism. This is the development of a language of expression that both mystics and scientists can understand, that links the two realms in a meaningful way, and that allows dialog to occur each on their own terms. Without this "common core" of agreed upon concepts and ideas there is no hope of bridging the gap, and no hope of eliminating the unnecessary problem of ineffability. Without a common language core people will still have their mystical experiences, as many as 1 in 2 people in this world by some estimates, but nobody will be able to talk about them, scientists will be unable to theorize and discuss them (except in a sideways fashion), and the silence and incommensurability will continue on.

Notably, developing a common language core, a set of concepts that scientists and mystics can use to talk about mystical experience and all that jazz, is what I have done not only in this book, but in my other books as well. I have developed a language and a conceptualization that I hope is science and mystic friendly, that allows the two sides to talk, and that will hopefully contribute to a "bridging of the gap" between the two. The language and definitions are interspersed throughout my writing, but I have been collecting the language and definitions at my SpiritWiki (http://www.thespiritwiki.com) for many years now. The work I am doing is still very much in progress and so definitions may change (slightly) and evolve over time. Current definitions of Lightning Path concepts are always available at the SpiritWiki and links are provided to SpiritWiki definitions throughout the entire corpus in order to ensure references to canonical definitions.

The **second reason** that mystical experiences remain locked behind a wall of ineffability and silence is simply that many scientists are hostile to mystical experience. They view it, in the best of cases, as biological epiphenomenon emerging from neurological process in the brains or, in the worst of cases, as lack of evolutionary development, pathology, or mindless superstition (Sosteric, 2013a). For this reason most scientists do not get anywhere near mystical experience. If they have them, they won't talk about them, and certainly won't use them as empirical data. If they are interested in them, they won't look at the experiences directly because they are too afraid of the potential fallout from colleagues. It is not an unreasonable fear since scientists have been excommunicated for daring to step too far outside the established ontological boxes (Freeman, 2005). To avoid the horrific experience of excommunication, most scientists will objectify the experience, quantify it, and study it in a "sideways" fashion (Sosteric, 2013a).[65] This is unfortunate

---

[65] I want to note at this point that I write under two names. I write under the pen name Michael Sharp, and I write under my real name Dr. Michael Sosteric. Writings under the pen name Michael Sharp are mystical writings. They are writings grounded in over a decade of my personal mystical experience and exploration of the hallways of consciousness. While in the middle of my decade long mystical explorations I intentionally avoided reading any book or article on any aspect of what I was going through. Everything I wrote was based on internal exploration. By contrast writings under my real name Dr. Sosteric are writings that are grounded in critical scholarly research and thinking. The works are kept separate primarily because the epistemological assumptions are entirely different. Sharp writings are grounded on an epistemology of inner experience. Truth in Sharp writings emerges from inner journeying and exploration. More to the point, Truth in Sharp writings emerges from direct connection with The Fabric of Consciousness (defined in the course of this volume one of The Book of Light). By contrast, Sosteric writings are grounded in scientific epistemologies that stress empirical evidence. Truth in Sosteric writings is a function of empirical support, logical sensibility, and rational plausibility. I have kept the two personas strictly separate for the past decade. The reasons for doing this are political and practical. Politically the separation allows me to keep the blood of spiritual experience away from the milk of scientific knowledge, thereby avoiding pre-emptive censure or defensive and fearful reaction. Practically the separation allowed me to think and work in peace and quiet, developing my thinking on its own grounds without the nattering buzzing of a science without language, and without the

since this sideways examination of mystical phenomenon violates the empirical core, the mystical revelation. When scientists approach the phenomenon with fear and misunderstanding, mystical revelation becomes about anything but mystical revelation. Not only that, but the mystical experiences themselves never get adequately analyzed or grounded. We talk about the sacred canopy (Berger, 1969), or the oceanic feeling (Freud, 1964), or the ineffable noesis (James, 1982; Stace, 1960), or the class nature of spirituality (Marx, 1978), or the externalizing process (Berger, 1999), or the community building functions (Durkheim, 1965 (1912)), to name just a few of the features, but we never talk about the mystical experiences themselves. We never ask whether they are valid, or how closely they represent reality, or anything. We can't even ask epistemological and methodological questions about the

---

confusing imposition of mysticism without proper grounding. Keeping them separate gave me a quiet intellectual space that allowed for careful examination of my own concepts, epistemology, and so on. The time for separation is over now I think. Now I am making efforts to merge the two. I am currently writing two books. One is entitled *The Sociology of Religion: A Mystical and Scientific Approach.* This book attempts to build a Sociology of Religion based on established sociological theory and research, and the mystical meanderings of Michael Sharp. Another, not yet named, attempts to develop a "spiritually sophisticated" psychology by building upon the foundation provided by Abraham Maslow and extending it with reference to current empirical work, and the mystical meanderings of Michael Sharp. It should be interesting.

experiences themselves, like how to distinguish a real one from a fake one, or how to assess the accuracy of the experience, or the purity of the expression, because we're too busy avoiding a direct stare. It is not our fault. Like the mystics themselves who lack the words and the concepts, we also lack the words and the concepts. We cannot talk sensibility, so we avoid. We are like the blindfolded men examining the elephant. We talk about this or that aspect of it but we never pull back to say "this is an elephant". It is unfortunate because until we take off the blindfold and look at the elephant, we'll not be making any sense at all.

So, how do we move beyond the erroneous attribution of ineffability to cosmic experiences? How do we collapse the gap between science and mysticism and move beyond the hostility?

How do we start talking about the elephant in the room?

Well, what is needed here is a scientist not afraid to dive into the mystical realms of oceanic consciousness, and not afraid to talk about them as such. This is what I have done. Over the past decade I have spent a lot of time in mystical reverie. I have spent a lot of time exploring and writing. I have welcomed the experiences as useful, and I have thought about the nature of the experiences and the nature of the knowledge gained. I have considered the psychology, sociology, and physics of the mystical realms and I have written [and plan to write more] books and student materials talking about mystical knowledge and mystical experience as such, and using said experiences as the groundwork for my LP corpus. As noted above, I have purposely avoided coming into contact

216

with other scientific writings on spirituality or mysticism, and mystical writings as such, during this period.[66] The strategy was simple. Avoiding other traditions and streams of knowledge forced me to build the foundation and the structure "in the clear," far away from confusing and ungrounded mystical conceptions and the dismissal and [sometimes] outright hostility of science.

The result of thinking about, writing about, and developing a language to talk about mystical experience is this book, and the Lightning Path corpus in general. In addition to being a straight ahead revelation of mystical truth, this book is a contribution towards recapturing mystical experience as a valid and respectable area of human inquiry. This book presents my mystical exploration of the cosmological and theological Truth of creation with a view towards creating a framework whereby anyone, scientists included, can look directly at mystical experience and examine it as such. In this book series I explored the mystical hallways of consciousness, asking questions as I progressed, and writing down the answers when I was satisfied that I had gotten them mostly right. In some cases, in particular in volume three where mystical revelation meets quantum physics, I checked what I was getting from The Fabric of Consciousness against what was known about quantum mechanics, sub-atomic particles,

---

[66] I did come into some contact with mystical writings, but it was always brief and cursory, more of a "quick evaluative glance" than a substantive and in depth analysis. It was all "at arm's length" you could say.

strings, and all that jazz, but this was only to identify words and concepts used in physics so that I could connect the dots. For the most part I developed my own frame of reference, my own conceptual rubric, my own terminology, and my own theoretical foundation.

I imagine a question that might arise at this point is "why go through all the time and effort to develop your own framework?" I did this, initially, and frankly, because I could not find suitable alternatives to encapsulate my revelatory noesis. Even cursory glances revealed glaring conceptual, theoretical, emotional, and psychological inadequacies. When compared against the information I was acquiring, most other systems appeared corrupted in some fashion. Concepts were misused or abused, original meanings were spun out of control, venal social and economic interests were imposed on otherwise interesting and potentially fruitful rubrics, and there was just too much baggage associated with the ideas and concepts for the concepts to be of any use at all. For example Jesus, one of the world's most famous and successful mystics, said a lot of interesting and valid things, but what others said about what he said, and what the Christian church said about what he said, obscures and blinds. His teachings have been used to justify everything from violent Feudal crusades to modern psychological and emotional abuse, and every point of violence in between. Or, take as another example the Western Tarot. In an article entitled *The Sociology of Tarot (Sosteric, 2013b)* I explore how a rather innocuous and mundane deck of playing cards, the Italian Tarot deck, got picked up by 18th century political and economic elites and spun into a "mystical tool" of class instruction and ideological indoctrination. At that time the old Feudal social order was collapsing and some sort of transitional idea was needed in order to lubricate the transition to new systems of elite control. In the hands of the Freemasons of the time the Tarot became one such tool. They created a mythology of spiritual mysticism and magic around the deck, imposed an elite ideology on the cards, and then handed the deck to people and said, more or less, "here, this is deep divine/spiritual/archetypal wisdom, and you should make it a part of your soul right now." And people did! Decker, Depaulis, and Dummett (1996, p. 27), the world's most eminent historian of Tarot, called the sum total of activity engaged in by cleric, priests, and Freemasons in the 18th through 20th centuries the:

> "...most successful propaganda campaign ever launched: not by a very long way the most important, but the most completely successful. An entire false history, and false interpretation, of the Tarot pack was concocted by the occultists; and it is all but universally believed." (Decker, Depaulis, & Dummett, 1996, p. 27).

The point of all this is simply this, it is hard to go to Christian teachings for a reflection of light, and it hard to go to esoteric systems as well.[67] We can even focus the problem right down

---

67 I have spent a lot of time attempting to strip the Western Tarot of its ideological associations, and a lot of time creating a new and authentic tool of spiritual awakening and empowerment based on

to individual concepts. Take the concept of sin,[68] for example. After a decade of exploration I think the concept of sin points to important aspects of mystical experience (Sharp, 2103b). Unfortunately it is very difficult to use the word "sin" in any sensible and scientifically friendly manner. For one thing, it is traditionally defined in moral and prescriptive terms, with references to authority to back it up. It is bad to commit a sin because "God" says so. This sort of statement doesn't fly, and rightly so, for a lot of people these days. For another, as soon as you say "sin" people get defensive, for different reasons. Refugees from Christianity will get defensive because of the judgment, shaming, and abuse that surrounds the term. Scientists will pooh-pooh the term as silly irrationality, and so on. Mention the word "sin" in a respectable academic conversation and you've almost guaranteed that everybody around you will stop listening. If you want to talk about "sin", or whatever important spiritual concepts it refers to, you have to either develop a new concept free of the thousands of years of crap and detritus, or you have to rehabilitate the term. In the case of the word "sin" I have tried to rehabilitate the term by defining sin as an action

---

the otherwise powerful imagery of the tarot. You can find that work in *The Book of the Triumph of Spirit*, *The Book of the Triumph of Spirit Master Key*, *The Book of the Triumph of Spirit: Healing and Activating with the Halo/Sharp System* and also summarized in the Halo/Sharp Lightning Path smartphone app.

[68] See http://www.thespiritwiki.com/index.php/Sin

committed by the physical unit[69] that is disjunctive[70] and out of alignment with higher consciousness, that causes serious (sometimes debilitating) emotional and psychological dissonance, and that harms another living being (Sharp, 2103b). In the case of other mystical ideas, like the nature of God, a new neutral term without emotional or psychological baggage was needed.

I imagine the question that arises at this point is **what kind of job** I have been doing while buried in the development of a conceptual rubric for talking about spirituality and mysticism. Put another way, have I provided enough so that all the blindfolded people examining the elephant can take their blindfolds off and finally begin talking about the beast as such? From my perspective I have been successful, even though at this time the program itself is barely half finished. I can see the potential success in a number of anecdotal evidentiary streams. **I can see it clearly in the fact that the Lightning Path corpus has not invalidated other perspectives.** In fact, quite the opposite. I have spoken directly, and sometimes recorded conversations, with Christians, Jews, Hindus, and others who report that far from being turned away from their traditions after exposure to the Lightning Path, they are turned on to the deep mystical value buried and obscured within. After exposure to Lightning Path teachings, they see the truth buried in the sacred texts,

---

[69] See http://www.thespiritwiki.com/index.php/Physical_Unit

[70] See http://www.thespiritwiki.com/index.php/Disjuncture

sometimes for the first time ever. This has occurred for various traditions, from Jewish mysticism rooted in the *Sepher Yezirah*, to Western Gnostic traditions rooted in Gnostic literature (Robinson, 1988) and alchemy (Holmyard, 1957 (1990)), to even Eastern religious perspectives. The truth in the systems comes into clear focus when viewed through the lens of the Lightning Path. Of course, there are issues. Not everything that is said in the ancient traditions remains valid, but just as the truth buried in the systems becomes obvious after exposure to LP concepts, so too does the falsity. After a certain degree of exposure, people see clearly what is of mystical value in their traditions, and what is not. LP allows an individual to separate the wheat from the chaff as it were. Of course, this is not exactly standard experimental proof, but it is suggestive. Even if it doesn't convince the scientists, it does convince the people themselves, and in the end getting the people to see the truth is what is most important.

The second line of evidence that I take to indicate I am doing at least a half decent job is my own academic work. As noted, up until quite recently I have avoided looking at mystical or religious traditions. I put my head down and worked in relative isolation. This was a conscious strategy and was designed to ensure that what I eventually wrote down would be based solely on my own mystical experiences, and my own analysis and interpretation of these experiences. I wanted the end result to be as pure as possible. This was scientifically and politically important. Politically, it helps keep the mystical knowledge unsullied. As noted elsewhere,[71] religion is an opportunistic corruption. Religion may universally start out rooted in the experience of mystics willing to talk, as William James (1982) said, but it gets corrupted along the way. Ruling classes pick up the deep cosmic insight of the mystic and use it to anesthetize the masses (Marx, 1970), or to create legitimizations and justifications of the ruling status quo (Berger, 1999). Opportunists pick it up and commercialize it (Carrette & King, 2008), or use it for political purposes (Butler, 2006). The whole history of religion is the history of religion and mysticism staring out as one thing, and becoming something entirely different. It starts out as being about the core experience,[72] but ends up something else.

In addition to keeping away from mystical and religious writings in general, I also kept away from the science of religion and mysticism as well, and much for the same reasons, that is to keep the system "pure" and to allow it to develop on its own foundations. As I noted above, except for a single instance of an academic being immersed in the world of mystical revelation (Castaneda, 1996), most academics, if

---

[71] In my Sociology of Religion course, taught as Dr. Mike Sosteric.

[72] If religion is like a tree and the roots of the tree are the mystic's experience, then we have seen the tree repeatedly cut down. When the tree is cut from the mystical roots, it dies just as surely as any planet dies. Obviously there are a lot of trees still out there, but they are artificial constructs and nothing more, plastic plants with only the most superficial resemblance to the mighty oak that stood there before. A little bit of lacquer and some creative lighting, and even tacky 70s kitsch can be made to appear as deep spiritual wisdom.

they look at all, look in a sideways sort of fashion (Sosteric, 2013a). The sideways look is useful as far as it goes, but the intellectualization of mystical experience imposes a frame of interpretation, a gestalt if you will, that blocks full appreciation of said mystical experience, and interferes with potentiality of experience. There is something to this. Whether we attribute the blockage to mediation of the frontal lobe (Freedman, Jeffers, Saeger, Binns, & Black, 2003), to difference in *assemblage points*,(Castaneda, 1996), or as I would argue simply unbalanced brain development coupled with spiritual mis-alignment and disjuncture, there is a different sensibility. Most scientists devote their entire life to tasks (like reading, writing, and arithmetic), that develop the left brain. Too much reading, writing, and arithmetic may make you a great thinker, a great theoretician, and a great systemizer, but they also undermine your ability to experience mystical/spiritual truth, and to apprehend that truth adequately. In the case of scientists and others, the required faculties may be quite undeveloped, even rankly immature.[73]

---

[73] Years ago I was watching Jill Taylor Taylor (2010) give her TED TALKS account of her trauma induced mystical experience. As she notes in that talk, her brain stroke shut down her left brain and opened space for her right brain to "speak freely," and it did. But listening to her right brain talk I was struck most powerfully by how childish and immature was her apprehension of her experience. It was if she was a seven year old child verbalizing about the wonder of a sunny day. At the time I figured that this was because her right brain was immature, even formerly suppressed. Why should this be so? People raised in a scientific milieu do not value the intuitive, soft, emotional, experiential side of things. They do not take time to develop this side. They even, for epistemological, ontological, and

This leaves scientists "without the eyes to see" as it were. [74] It leaves the blindfold on and confines them to talking about parts of the elephant, rather the elephant as a whole. This is not a bad thing. A lot of interesting things have been written about mystical experience by scientists. But their theories, conceptualizations, and analysis are always limited by the intellectualized view. Staying away from the science of mysticism was a way to avoid the "corrupting influence" of this intellectualized view. [75] Staying away from both mystical

---

professional reasons (i.e. it might undermine their legitimacy in the eyes of their colleagues), actively suppress it. This essentially puts a lead cover over the right brain itself, locks it away from experience, and confines it to childhood levels of development. Like childhood trauma and lack of need satisfaction may stunt your emotional growth, childhood suppression of the right brain and subsequent biased development of the left may lock you in childhood levels of mystical sensibility. It is a common problem. Many people listening to Taylor speak were impressed with her characterization of her mystical experience, but I wasn't. It was like listening to your average ten year old child trying to explain complicated quantum mechanics, or the deep psychological processes of defense mechanism, with a child's level of development. The difference was, it wasn't so much cute as painful to watch. It was impressive only to other "children", and in a way damaging to the cause. Taylor and others present her experience as leading to enlightenment but really it amounts to borderline expression, and childish solipsistic failure. It makes mystics look bad, and gives a false impression of the nature of mystical experience.

[74] William James (1982) was keenly interested in mystical experiences, and open to them. Despite this fact he went his entire life without having an authentic mystical revelation. Such is the price we pay for unbalanced hemispheric development.

[75] The difficulties go both ways. People with overdeveloped right

writing and scientific writing forced me to appreciate the mystical insight, and build the system on its own terms.

I recognize at this point that what I am saying is anathema to science. Scientists do not start from the beginning. Scientists stake their career, and their life, by standing on the back of giants. A scientist starting at the beginning of mystical experience is like a scientist stepping back to Galileo. Does it open you up to bias and solipsism? Does it make any sense at all? I think yes, and yes. It is a dangerous approach, but it does make sense, and for the reasons outlined above and more. Although I do wish to discuss the methods and epistemology in more detail at a later date, I would like to point out that now, as I jump back in to the academic, experiential, and religious literature. From Castenada to Kaballah I am finding strong correspondences between what I have written and what is already out there. Not only that, but I find that I understand these systems as well. This correspondence and understanding is, for me, strong conformation that the concepts, ideas, and rubric I have been developing are successful, true, and potentially quite productive. I can "see" the nature of mystical writing, the truth being represented, the failures in linguistic

---

brains and atrophied left brains have similar difficulties. They may apprehend the entire elephant, but they have trouble appreciating the entity, and grounding their insights. This leads, in normal cases, to lack of conceptual rigor, two-dimensional characterizations, and solipsistic conceptualizations meaningful only to the mystic themselves. When it comes to filtering their experiences through the left brain alone they appear just as "left-brain" childish and immature as Jill Taylor appeared right-brain childish and immature.

conceptualization involved (see my notes on "Abraham's struggle" above), and so on. The preliminary foray into the mystical and scientific literature leaves me with the impression that what I have done is created a way of looking at the elephant that allows us to take the blindfold off and look at the beast for the first time in the clear light of day. Of course, I know this is a big claim, and know there is a lot of work to do on this, but I would like to say four things before closing up this preface.

One, the conceptual framework is not all contained in this book series. It exists elsewhere in my writings, in books I've written under the mystical rubric, in the creation of the SpiritWiki,[76] and in LP teachings materials designed to teach people how to have mystical experience. This book series is focused primarily on theology and cosmology. It answers the big questions about the nature of god, the nature of creation, the relationship between the two, and your place in the whole shebang. It is not meant to stand alone nor, as we shall see, is it meant as an acceptable academic summary of my "mystical" position. It was written in the first instance to express and ground mystical experience and it must be appreciated on those terms, or not at all.[77]

---

[76] See http://www.thespiritwiki.com/

[77] **Methodological note:** This is not to say that we engage in solipsistic and groundless self-referential mysticism, of the type the Castaneda advocates (Castaneda, 1996). I am applying a methodology here. The adequacy of my account of creation can evaluated by a) checking its correspondence with other systems, b)

Second, the program is far from complete. At the time of this writing I estimate I am only half way through it all. I still have a lot of theoretical and conceptual work to do. I have to complete the cosmology and theology of this Book of Light, I have to finish the development of teaching materials, and I have to discuss and present the entire corpus to the scientific establishment. I've been working on the first two for a while but I've only begun to do the third. At this time the plan is to develop two university level courses (A Sociology of Religion I and a Sociology of Religion II), find a suitable journal outlet (or outlets), and also to write two books, one on the Sociology of Religion and one developing a spiritually sophisticated psychology. At the time of this writing I am about one chapter into both of those books. As you can see, there is still a lot of work to do. I say this here only to point out to anybody who

---

checking it against your own mystical experience, c) seeing if the information provided provides a pathway to your own mystical revelations, d) assessing its fit with what is known in psychology, sociology, physics, chemistry, and so on and e) determining whether or not "following the path" or listening to the advice and perspectives leads to enhanced mental, emotional, and psychological health. I'll have more to say about the epistemology and methodology of mysticism at a later date. Suffice it to note at this point that all this is in line with what William James methodological advice, taken from that Bible that we should judge religious and mystical experience by the fruits. "By their fruits ye shall know them" (James, 1982: 20). Although in this case we leave behind the Christian undertones, and the fear of origin, and refer to neutral empirical criteria. Also see (Sharp, 2010) for a list of evaluative criteria (the seven pillars of authentic spirituality) that can be used to judge the "authenticity" of a specific implementation of the various religious/spiritual traditions.

may be interested in exploring the academic side that that the map isn't quite ready and if you are serious about finding out more, you should probably make me the first point of contact into the system.

Third, because of the size of the program, and because the first decade of development I was locked away in solipsistic consideration of my own mystical experience, inevitably I will make mistakes.[78] I have been sensitive to this in the past and have endeavored to fix these as identified. In fact, the entire LP corpus is open to ongoing revision. This volume will evolve over time as will other LP materials, and none of the materials should be considered absolutely fixed. Those with specialized knowledge of chemistry, physics, psychology, etc.

---

[78] I should note here that even though I did make my experience the reference point for the development of this corpus, nevertheless I did have, even from the start, certain epistemological standards. I didn't just puke mystical wisdom onto the page as so many do, take it as divine revealed knowledge, and then trundle off to the local pub for a drink while generations struggle to understand. I brought a scientific sensibility, reliance on rational thought and logic, and the intent to present "the truth and nothing but." In other words, I brought my left brain with me and used that to develop, refine, and vet my "mystical wisdom." I vetted revelation against what I already knew about psychology, sociology, physics, chemistry, and so on. I vetted revelation against common sense. Finally, I vetted revelation against the impact of the teachings on others. I used, and continue to use, reader feedback and criticism just like a software programmer uses bug reports to improve software. The result is the iterative, and laborious, development of what I would call an authentic spiritual pathway. The goal of all this was not just sensible and grounded revelation, but a working pathway to enlightenment and empowerment (or activation as I call it).

should feel free to assist the development of this work by, among other things, contributing their expertise in the form of supportive advice and corrections. If I get something wrong, or if I say something that violates some known aspect of empirical reality, tell me, politely and in a non-aggressive manner, and I will endeavor to take it into account and incorporate it.

Fourth, and finally, the task that looms ahead is a big task not only for me, but for others as well. There is a lot of conceptual mapping that needs to be done, a lot of conceptual revision, a lot of careful analysis, and a lot of effort aimed at extending the theoretical foundation and providing an empirical program. Not only that, but there may be a lot of healing and psychotherapy needed as well. One of the principles of LP psychology is that our current socialization processes are violent, abusive, misconceived, insensitive to the true nature of the physical unit as a sensitive instrument, highly evolved vehicle for consciousness (Sharp, 2103a), biased in favor of left-brain development, and pre-emptive of mystical experience. More to the point, the world we live in encourages a certain level of functional development, creates a certain type of psychic constellation, and boxes and limits you based on your particular class position and class background. This is done, basically, by damaging the physical unit. Not too much of course, because the owners of the world need workers, managers, and CEOs, but just enough to undermine, more or less, the ability of the physical unit to connect and focus consciousness. There is a "hidden" class curriculum in our societies and schools (Anyon, 1980) and this class based curriculum shuts us down, bottles us up, and leaves us with psychological, emotional, and spiritual deficits. I would vociferously state, and underline with persistent conviction, that assessing accurately a mystic's transmission, and even providing accurate mystical knowledge, is a function of emotional health, psychological stability, development of rational facilities, consistent and long term connection with The Fabric of Consciousness, and persistent effort aimed at "getting to the bottom" of the experiences. In the above list I would emphasize emotional health and psychological stability. You need to be healthy and whole if you want to work, much less experience, in this area. This may seem a startling statement, but I'm not the first one to make it. Maslow (1954, p. 10) suggested that scientists needed to be happy, psychologically healthy, and have their needs satisfied in order to have the energy and perspective necessary to be able to accurately assess truth. He even went so far as to recommend psychotherapy for scientists to ensure mental and emotional stability, and I would do the same. There is nothing weak, watered down, impotent, anemic, or wishy-washy about the consciousness that underlines mystical experience. In fact, exactly the opposite is true. Thus, full apprehension of consciousness requires more than just psychological, emotional, and spiritual health, it requires psychological, emotional, and spiritual strength. One is not born with this strength; it must be nurtured and developed just as one nurtures and develops language, artistic talent, or business acumen. In the vast majority of cases these strengths are, however, not nurtured but undermined by the toxic socialization process of this planet. In those cases healing the physical unit (body and mind) becomes, like it or not, a first step towards serious exploration and work in this area.

Citations

Anyon, J. (1980). Social Class and the Hidden Curriculum of Work. *Journal of Education, 162*(1).

Berger, P. (1969). The Sacred Canopy: Elements of a Sociological Theory of Religion. New York: Anchor Books.

Berger, P. (1999). The Descularization of the World: Resurgent Religion and World Politics. Grand Rapids MI: Eerdmans.

Butler, J. (2006). *Born Again: The Christian Right Globalized.* New York: Pluto Press.

Carrette, J., & King, R. (2008). *Selling Spirituality: The Silent Takeover of Religion.* New York: Routledge.

Castaneda, C. (1996). The Teachings of Don Juan: A Yaqui Way of Knowledge, 40th Anniversary Edition. New York: Washington Square Press.

Chen, Z., Qi, W., Hood, R. W., & Watson, P. J. (2011). Common Core Thesis and Qualitative and Quantitative Analysis of Mysticism in Chinese Buddhist Monks and Nuns. [Article]. *Journal for the Scientific Study of Religion, 50*(4), 654-670. doi: 10.1111/j.1468-5906.2011.01606.x

Decker, R., Depaulis, T., & Dummett, M. (1996). *A Wicked Pack of Cards: The Origins of the Occult Tarot.* New York: St Martin's Press.

Don, N. S. (2010). Electrical Activity in the Brain and the Extraordinary Mind. In H. L. Friedman & S. Krippner (Eds.), *Mysterious Minds: The Neurobiology of Psychics, Mediums, and Other Extraordinary People* (pp. 113-127). Santa Barbara, California: Praeger.

Dummett, M., Decker, R., & Depaulis, T. (1996). *A Wicked Pack of Cards: Origins of the Occult Tarot*. London: Bristol Classical Press.

Durkheim, E. (1965 (1912)). *The Elementary Forms of Religious Life*. New York: Free Press.

Freedman, M., Jeffers, S., Saeger, K., Binns, M., & Black, S. (2003). Effects of Frontal Lobe Lesions on Intentionality and Random Physical Phenomenon. *Journal of Scientific Exploration, 17*, 651-668.

Freeman, A. (2005). The Sense of Being Glared At: What is it LIke to be a Heretic? *Journal of Consciousness Studies, 12*(6), 4-9.

Freud, S. (1964). *The Future of an Illusion*. New York: Anchor Books.

Hegel, G. W. F. (2004). *The Philosophy of History*. New York: Dover Publications.

Holmyard, E. J. (1923). The Emerald Tablet. *Nature, 112*, 525-526. doi: 0.1038/112525a0

Holmyard, E. J. (1957 (1990)). *Alchemy*. New York: Dover Publications.

James, W. (1982). The Varieties of Religious Experience: A Study of Human Nature. New York: Penguin.

Kalisch, I. (2006 (1877)). *Sepher Yezirah: A Book on Creation*. San Diego: The Book Tree.

Marx, K. (1970). A Contribution to the Critique of Hegel's Philosophy of Right. Cambridge: Cambridge University Press.

Marx, K. (1978). The German Ideology. In R. Tucker (Ed.), *The Marx-Engels Reader*. New York: Norton.

Robinson, J. M. (Ed.). (1988). The Nag Hammadi Library: The Definitive new Translation of the Gnostic Scriptures (Third ed.). San Francisco: HarperSanFrancisco.

Roll, W. G., & Williams, B. J. (2010). Quantum Theory, Neurobiology, and Parapsychology. In H. L. Friedman & S. Krippner (Eds.), *Mysterious Minds: The Neurobiology of Psychics, Mediums, and Other Extraordinary People* (pp. 1-35). Santa Barbara, California: Praeger.

Sharp, M. (2007). The Great Awakening: Concepts and Techniques for Successful Spiritual Practice. St. Albert, Alberta, Canada: Lightning Path Press.

Sharp, M. (2010). *The Rocket Scientists' Guide to Authentic Spirituality*. St. Albert, Alberta: Lightning Path Press.

Sharp, M. (2103a). *Lightning Path Core Lesson Package* (Vol. 2). St. Albert, Alberta: Lightning Path Press.

Sharp, M. (2103b). *Lightning Path Intermediate Module A - Foundations* (Vol. 3). St. Albert, Alberta: Lightning Path Press.

Sosteric, M. (2013a). The Sociology of Religion - An Introduction. St. Albert, Alberta: Socjourn.

Sosteric, M. (2013b). A Sociology of Tarot. *Unpublished*.

Stace, W. T. (1960). *Mysticism and Philosophy*. London: Macmillan.

Taylor, J. B. (2010). My Stroke of Insight: A Brain Scientist's Personal Journey. New York: Plume.

Index

About the Author

Michael Sharp is a Sociologist with a specialization in psychology, religion, occult studies, social inequality, scholarly communication, and critical theory. After a dramatic crown chakra opening caused him to question the materialist foundation of modern science, he began exploring the spiritual and mystical side of life. Recognizing early the presence of elitism and patriarchy in the world's religious and "secret" traditions, he began creating a new, open system of mysticism free of the opportunistic bias in "old energy" systems. The Lightning Path™ is the culmination of his research and work. Visit Michael at www.michaelsharp.org.

About the Lightning Path

The Lightning Path (or simply LP for short) is an intellectual, emotional, psychological, and spiritual system of awakening and empowerment (a "mystery school" if you like, but without all the useless mystery) designed to help you get of the sinking ship of the old world and make "the shift" into an awakened, activated, and ascended state of existence. It is sophisticated, powerful, logical, grounded, rational, intellectually and metaphorically rigorous, politically sophisticated, empirically verifiable, authentic, effective, and accessible to everyone regardless of race, class, or gender. No requirements are set for entry and no judgments are made in passage.

The Lightning Path is organized into various levels or "grades." LP teachings start at the Core level and move through Intermediate, Advanced, Mentor, and Post-secondary levels of study.

- For more information or to purchase the next LP grade level please visit www.thelightningpath.com or http://www.thelightningpath.com/shop/lp-study-packages/

- To become a student of the LP and get access to all study packages, books, supporting materials, articles, audio, and so forth, visit

http://www.thelightningpath.com/register/

- To download the Lightning Path introductory booklet for free, visit http://www.thelightningpath.com/gifts/

www.ingramcontent.com/pod-product-compliance
Lightning Source LLC
Chambersburg PA
CBHW051822040426
42447CB00006B/320